Sex, Love, and Marriage— A Celebration

Sex, Love, and Marriage— A Celebration

The Song of Solomon

JONATHAN F. BAYES

RESOURCE *Publications* • Eugene, Oregon

SEX, LOVE, AND MARRIAGE—A CELEBRATION
The Song of Solomon

Copyright © 2012 Jonathan F. Bayes. All rights reserved. Except for brief quotations in critical publications or reviews, no part of this book may be reproduced in any manner without prior written permission from the publisher. Write: Permissions, Wipf and Stock Publishers, 199 W. 8th Ave., Suite 3, Eugene, OR 97401.

Resource Publications
An Imprint of Wipf and Stock Publishers
199 W. 8th Ave., Suite 3
Eugene, OR 97401
www.wipfandstock.com

ISBN 13: 978-1-61097-676-3
Manufactured in the U.S.A.

The text of the Song of Solomon reproduced here is a hybrid, borrowing from various versions. Unless otherwise stated, all other Scripture citations are from the New King James Version of the Bible © 1982 by Thomas Nelson, Inc., Nashville, Tennessee.

To Cathy—the best wife in the world.

Contents

List of Abbreviations / ix

1   Sexually Explicit / 1

2   Love—Powerful, Passionate, Priceless
    (Song of Solomon 8:6b–7) / 9

3   An Impressionistic Song Cycle / 14

4   Wrinkles and Palaces
    (Song of Solomon 1) / 17

5   Wonders and Warnings
    (Song of Solomon 2) / 28

6   Desperation and Satisfaction
    (Song of Solomon 3) / 40

7   Sense and Sensibility
    (Song of Solomon 4:1—5:1) / 50

8   Realism and Resolution
    (Song of Solomon 5:2—6:10) / 63

9   The Joy of Sex
    (Song of Solomon 6:11—7:12) / 74

10 Inseparable Togetherness
    (Song of Solomon 7:13—8:6a) / 85

11 Royalty for Everyone
    (Song of Solomon 8:8–14) / 93

Bibliography / 99

List of Abbreviations

Translations of the Song of Solomon used

ANT   *The Song of Songs: A New Translation*, by Ariel Bloch and Chana Bloch (Berkeley and Los Angeles: University of California Press, 1995).

BBE   *Bible in Basic English*, translated by Samuel Henry Hooke, 1949.

ESV   *English Standard Version*, published by HarperCollins Publishers © 2001, by Crossway Bibles, a division of Good News Publishers, Wheaton, Illinois.

GNB   *Good News Bible (Today's English Version)*, published by Collins/Fontana © 1976, American Bible Society, New York.

GW   *God's Word®*, published by Baker Publishing Group © 1995, God's Word to the Nations, Grand Rapids, Michigan.

HBE   *The Hebrew Bible in English*, published 1917 by the Jewish Publication Society, Philadelphia, Pennsylvania.

HCSB   *Holman Christian Standard Bible®* Copyright © 2003, Holman Bible Publishers, Nashville, Tennessee.

JB   *Jubilee Bible*, translated by Russel Stendal, 2000.

KJV   *Authorised King James Version* (1611). Note: where

Translations of the Song of Solomon used

I have used the KJV I have updated the language to eliminate obsolete grammatical forms such as "thou," "feedest,," etc.

LB   *The Living Bible*, paraphrased by Kenneth Taylor © 1974, Coverdale House Publishers, London and Eastbourne.

MSG   *The Message*, published by Eugene H. Peterson © 2002, NavPress Publishing Group, Colorado Springs, Colorado.

NASB   *New American Standard Bible*, published by Moody Press © 1973, The Lockman Foundation, Chicago, Illinois.

NEB   *New English Bible*, published by Oxford University Press and Cambridge University Press © 1972, The British and Foreign Bible Society, London.

NIV   *New International Version*, published by Hodder and Stoughton © 1980, New York International Bible Society, East Brunswick, New Jersey.

NKJV   *New King James Version* © 1994, Thomas Nelson, Inc., Nashvilee, Tennessee.

orig   *Original*. Lines so marked are my own translation.

REB   *Revised English Bible* © 1992, Oxford University Press, New York.

RIL   *An English Translation of the Jewish Bible* by Rabbi Isaac Leeser, 1853.

RSV   *Revised Standard Version*, published by Oxford University Press © 1952, by Division of Christian Education of the National Council of the Churches of Christ in the United States of America, New York.

RV   *Revised Version*, published by Cambridge University Press, 1885.

Translations of the Song of Solomon used

WBC   Translation in *Word Biblical Commentary, Vol. 23B: Song of Songs and Lamentations* by Duane Garrett (Dallas: Word, 2004).

YLT   *Young's Literal Translation,* by Robert Young, 1862.

1

Sexually Explicit

BOOK CLUB CATALOGS OFTEN contain a section headed *Erotica*. Certain books in that section are said to be "sexually explicit." When you see those words you usually take them to be a warning: here is a book to avoid. Such books, we assume, are sordid. They represent a corruption of human passion, a distortion of sexual pleasure.

But we must face this fact: if we were to arrange the books of the Bible into categories, we should have to put the Song of Solomon into the section headed *Erotica*. The Song is sexually explicit. That does not mean that it is sordid. It is beautiful. It does not represent the corruption of human passion. It is a joyful affirmation of physical love. It does not portray the distortion of sexual pleasure. As we read the Song of Solomon God invites us to join him in celebrating sexual love.

The difference is obvious. Modern "sexually explicit" books use pictures to titillate lust. The Song of Solomon uses words, inspired by God, to arouse appreciation of one of God's most pleasant gifts to the human race.

The Song of Solomon is definitely a difficult book. Its sexually explicit nature has sometimes been an embarrassment to devout readers. There has been a tendency to feel that decency forbids us from talking about these things in an open way. So some people have seen the Song as pure allegory. This is true both of Christian interpretation, and of Jewish interpretation going back to the time before the coming of Christ. They claim that it is not really about human love at all. That seems to be the surface meaning, but it is totally irrelevant. The real meaning, so the argument goes, is hidden. The Song of Solomon is actually about, and only about, the love between God and his people, or between Christ and believers.

But there is a real problem with this approach. Anyone can find any hidden meaning that they want to. If we disregard the obvious meaning, then who knows where we might end up and what fancy ideas we might invent?

Professor John Murray was a minister of the Free Church of Scotland who went over to the States to teach at Westminster Theological Seminary. In 1983 a passage from a letter he had written about the Song of Solomon was quoted in the Free Church magazine. This is what he said:

> I cannot now endorse the allegorical interpretation of the Song of Solomon. I think the vagaries of interpretation given in terms of the allegorical principle indicate that there are no well-defined hermeneutical canons to guide us in determining the precise meaning and application if we adopt the allegorical view.[1]

To put it more simply, what Professor Murray is saying is this. When you have to find a hidden meaning in the Song of Solomon, when you argue that what the book seems to be saying it isn't saying at all, you end up with a huge variety of interpretations, some of which are very comical. This simply proves that no rules exist for finding out what the Song really means, if you treat it as an allegory. You can make it mean anything you want. You are then on dangerous ground. There is no way of knowing whether you have wandered into serious error.

---

1. Free Church of Scotland, "John Murray," 52.

So it's much better to take the Song of Solomon at face value. It is a sexually explicit celebration (though not an indecent one) of the love between a man and a woman as God the Creator intended it to be within the context of marriage. It is an invitation to rejoice with God in the pleasure which he has built into human life and relationships.

Having said that, of course, we do know that human love in the bond of marriage is intended by God as a visual aid to help us understand something of the love between Christ and the church. In Ephesians 5:22–33 the apostle talks about the relationship between husband and wife, but in verse 32 he writes, "This is a great mystery, but I speak concerning Christ and the church". In that passage teaching about human marriage and teaching about the relationship between Christ and the church are intricately interwoven. This is not surprising, because human love is patterned on the love that Christ has for the church. So when you look at a marriage, particularly a Christian marriage which is functioning well, you can see a beautiful picture of how Christ and his church are in love with each other. There are many other places in the Bible too where the relationship between God and his people is described in terms of the sexual union of a man with his wife. Most notable is the Old Testament prophet Hosea.

This means that it would be very foolish to say that the Song of Solomon has nothing to do with the love of God for his people or of Christ for believers. Indeed, the very fact that the Song is a celebration of human loving drives us on to hear in its singing the new song of joyful union between the Lord Jesus Christ and his beloved bride, the church. John Murray agrees. Having rejected the allegorical interpretation of the Song, the quotation given above continues like this:

> However, I also think that in terms of biblical analogy the Song could be used to illustrate the relation of Christ to his church. The marriage bond is used in Scripture as a pattern of Christ and the church. If the Song portrays marital love and relationship on the highest levels

of exercise and devotion, then surely it may be used to exemplify what is transcendently true in the bond that exists between Christ and the church.[2]

However, you can't hear that love song between Christ and his people, unless you have first listened properly to Solomon's love song on the purely human plane. From there we are led upwards to a higher level where we can appreciate something of heavenly love.

But that doesn't mean that the love described on the human level is just a slightly embarrassing necessity to get us up on to that higher plane. The human love story is not an unfortunate hurdle which we have to get over in order to hear the music of that "love divine, all loves excelling."

The truth is that the Song of Solomon works both ways. The human love song does indeed point to that greatest love in all eternity—"the Son of God, who loved me and gave himself for me" (Galatians 2:20). But then the very fact that the Bible paints this picture of divine love in terms of the love between a man and his wife sends us back down to earth again. We recognise that there is absolutely nothing sordid or dirty about a sexual relationship between a woman and her husband in that proper context of marriage. It is, in fact, something to be celebrated, to rejoice in, to enter into with impassioned pleasure. Enjoying the fun of sex is part of the life which comes to us as a love gift from our Creator. So as we read the Song of Solomon, the human love story points us upwards to God's love. And then, thinking about that, we are brought down to earth again to celebrate human love.

I wonder whether it struck you as you read the previous paragraph that I referred to the sexual relationship between "a woman and her husband." I could have said "a man and his wife," but I wrote it as I did quite deliberately. The reason is that as a matter of fact the Song of Solomon does give greater prominence to the woman than the man. On my calculation, the woman

---

2. Free Church of Scotland, "John Murray," 52.

Sexually Explicit

speaks 224 lines, and her husband just 148. The woman is far more prominent than the man in this love song.

Maybe that's deliberate. It has been a sad tragedy of human societies in general that women have been downtrodden, under the thumb of men. Sometimes that has been true in a specific home. The man has been a domineering husband, and the woman's personality has been squashed and destroyed. That is an example of how the male leadership which God has appointed has become corrupted and abused by sin, as sin corrupts and abuses everything. Male leadership has been turned into male power, often cruelly exercised.

Perhaps, by reversing the prominence of women and men Solomon is seeking to redress the balance. Maybe it's an example of what today would be called "positive discrimination." It is not aiming merely to turn the tables and give the woman a position of dominance over men. Rather, it is asserting the equality of man and woman in the union of love as created by God.

Our society has tried to take a stand against male abuse of women. But recently I heard a woman who lectures in Women's Studies at Sussex University speaking on the radio. She was complaining that things have gone too far. Men, she said, are becoming frightened of taking normal initiatives towards women for fear that they are going to be accused of sexual harassment. It's just an example of how we sinful human beings always mess things up. We see something wrong. We try to put it right, and end up creating another wrong. That's the way sin goes.

But the Bible avoids that pitfall. The picture that we get from the Song of Solomon, although the woman is prominent, is one of overflowing joy which the woman and the man share together, harmoniously. In their union with each other both are enjoying the whole business. And that is what Solomon is commending to us in all our marriages—unity, equality, harmony, joy.

Who are the wife and her husband in the Song of Solomon? Quite a few different answers have been given. I shall simply state my own view. Readers who are interested may look up other views in the commentaries. I think the happy couple are Solomon himself and his wife, probably Pharaoh's daughter. She was Solomon's first wife (1 Kings 3:1). Solomon is referred to several times in the book, and in 3:7–11 he seems to be one of the main characters. The name "Shulamite," which describes the woman in 6:13, has been variously interpreted. The most likely explanation, to my mind, is that it is simply the feminine form of "Solomon." That is not obvious in English, although even in translation both names contain an *s*, an *l* and an *m*. We can at least see the similarity there. In Hebrew the consonants are exactly the same. The only difference is the vowels. The name "Solomon" contains the vowels which normally indicate the masculine gender. The name "Shulamite" contains the vowels which normally indicate the feminine gender. So, in modern talk, I think "Shulamite" could be translated "Mrs. Solomon." That's simply what it means.

However, the main thing is that the relationship between Solomon and the Shulamite is being used as an example of sexual love, to which every couple may aspire.

From what we know of Solomon's love life the picture which he paints in this song is clearly rather idealised. 1 Kings 11:1 says, "But King Solomon loved many foreign women as well as the daughter of Pharaoh." It goes on to describe how all these foreign women turned his heart away from the LORD.

I imagine that Solomon wrote the Song late in life when he had an opportunity to look back on the way he'd lived. It caused him great regret. Now he wants to teach others to avoid his mistakes. In reality, I suspect, Solomon missed out on the potential joy of a deeply loving marriage, because he'd taken all these other women as well. But now, in composing this song towards the end of his life, he admits, wistfully, what might have been. If only! He is inspired to describe what God intended, as if to say to us all: aim at this; don't do what I did. Then your life will be a permanent celebration of joy.

So I think we are looking at a love song which is sung between Solomon and his wife. But just at the end, from 8:12,

Sexually Explicit

another couple seem to speak up. Another man speaks to Solomon. He says, "My own vineyard is before me. You, O Solomon, may have a thousand, and those who keep its fruit two hundred". And the implication is, "So what if you have? My own vineyard is before me." Here is someone who doesn't have the riches of a Solomon, the thousands of pounds (or whatever the equivalent was in those days), but who, nonetheless, enjoys his own love relationship with his own wife. That's what he means. It's a picture, "my own vineyard."

So in the end, for all their royal splendor, Solomon and Shulamite (Mrs. Solomon) are just ordinary human beings. And this new voice chipping in at the end seems to say to us that every couple in the world may enjoy the kind of relationship described here. You don't have to be a king. You don't have to be the daughter of a king. Sexual joy in marriage is God's gift to all people. And sexual love is something worth celebrating.

I need at this point to say a word about the translation of the Song. Some lines or phrases are very hard to understand, and there is a wide variety of different possible translations. Sometimes I have preferred one translation, sometimes another. Sometimes my preference is based on the conclusion that one translation is slightly more accurate than others. Sometimes, there is nothing to choose between translations on the ground of accuracy, but I have made a subjective judgement that one translation is more fitting, more vivid, more poetic than others. I am therefore printing each section in my own hybrid translation. A footnote will indicate the source of my preferred rendering. Where a number of versions agree on the translation I have simply listed one representative version. Occasionally I have offered my own translation of a line. This will be indicated in the footnote by the abbreviation "orig."

One thing which is difficult in interpreting the Song of Solomon is to know at any point who is speaking and to whom. In many Bibles the editors have tried to help us by allocating some verses to Shulamite (the wife), others to the Beloved (the husband), and others to further participants in the drama. Those headings are not inspired. They are not present in the original text. They have been added to help us to make sense of the book. However, not everyone agrees on exactly how the verses should be allocated, so you find some differences between different Bibles. I have come to a different conclusion from the editors of some of our English translations of the Song. I shall not therefore include headings with my translation, but shall indicate at the beginning of my exposition of each section how I think that the words should be allocated. I also differ from the editors of some translations, in that I am persuaded that, apart from the second half of the final chapter, the wedding scenes in 3:6–11 and the first two lines of 8:5, and the last two lines of 5:1, there are only two characters in the Song, Shulamite and Solomon. I shall amplify this comment as we proceed.

Let me at this point make one very important comment. As we study the Song of Solomon we won't be able to dodge those parts which are sexually explicit. But where the Song differs from pornographic literature is that it's not crude, it's not offensive. It is written decently and tastefully. The problem with the world in which we live is that sex is abused. It is used sinfully. But the Song of Solomon is not describing that context. It is describing the proper context of marriage. So as we look at the teaching of this song we shall try to be decent and reticent, and not crude and offensive. But at the same time we must not be embarrassed to hear what Solomon is really saying to us. Come and join in celebrating sexual love!

2

Love—Powerful, Passionate, Priceless

(Song of Solomon 8:6b–7)

IN THE HEBREW BIBLE the Song of Solomon is included in the "Wisdom Literature." This category includes the books of Job, Proverbs and Ecclesiates as well. Their main aim is to teach us about human life and human experience in the light of the basic truth that *God is*. They are talking about how we understand human life, given that God is the Creator and the ever-present Lord in his creation. The question which they set out to answer is, how can we make sense of our experience? After all, as Job tells us, there are times when it just doesn't make sense, or doesn't seem to. What is life all about? What things really matter? How can we know God?

Well, one aspect of our human experience in the light of God's reality is the love of a man for a woman. But the Song of Solomon is a bit different from most of the Wisdom Literature, in that it is a poem. It is a song. Most of it is an illustration. It is describing a relationship, not giving us ground rules for relationships, except in so far as we can work them out from what is actually happening in the love between this man and this woman. There is only one exception to that. There is just a verse and a half in the whole of the Song of Solomon where it seems that a narrator speaks. Just for a moment we are not looking in to this particular relationship between Solomon and Shulamite, but hearing a general statement about love. That is in the last chapter, the second half of verse 6 and verse 7, where it says this:

> **6B** For love is as powerful as death,
> Its jealousy unyielding as the grave;
> Even its sparks are a raging fire,
> A most vehement flame.
> **7** Many waters cannot quench love,
> No flood can sweep it away.
> If someone were to offer for love
> All the wealth in his house,
> He would be utterly despised.[1]

This is where we begin. Here is a reflection on the nature of love. All the rest of the book illustrates and celebrates love. But here is a statement about love. This statement is the key to the whole book. All the rest illustrates the truth of it. In making this declaration about love Solomon is inviting us to celebrate, to rejoice in the experience of love which is given to us by God. This short passage teaches three things.

LOVE IS POWERFUL

"Love is as powerful as death." Death is inescapable. It overpowers everybody in the end, from the lowest to the greatest. Cleverness won't protect you from death. Money won't preserve you from death. Position can't insure you against death.

In the same way, love is a universal human reality. There is a driving power within us. God has made us to love. Once our heart is conquered, love overpowers us. However manly we may be, love is irresistible. It's just part of the way we are as human beings.

---

1. V. 6b, line 1 GNB, line 2 NIV, line 3 ANT, line 4 NKJV; v. 7, lines 1–2 NEB, lines. 3–4, REB, line 5 ESV.

This of course points us to God. We are made in God's image, and when the Son of God came into the world to save lost and hopeless sinners, he was overpowered by love. That's what drove him to give himself on the cross.

That being so, we have no reason for shame when the urge to love our husband/our wife takes possession of us. It is simply a reflection of the Creator who made us.

Solomon points out that the power of love is expressed in jealousy. He describes jealousy as a raging fire, a vehement flame. Here is the possessiveness which is an essential part of true love. The sense of rage if love is betrayed is quite right and proper. God himself said, "You shall have no other gods before me . . . for I, the LORD your God, am a jealous God" (Exodus 20:3, 5). God will have his people for himself. He will be affronted when they go after other gods. And in just the same way, when a man and a woman have been united in love, there will be outrage if one or other breaks that bond. A love which does not have that jealousy about it is a very weak and wimpish sort of love, and hardly worthy of the name.

The apostle Paul spoke to the Corinthians about his jealousy for them. He says, "I have betrothed you to one husband" (2 Corinthians 11:2). The preaching of the gospel had resulted in their being married to Christ. So Paul says, I'm jealous that you remain faithful.

Jealousy, we are told, is "unyielding as the grave." In Proverbs 30:16 the grave is listed as one of four things that never say, "It is enough." The other three are the barren womb, the earth that is not satisfied with water, and the fire. A fire will keep burning as long as there are things to burn. The earth will never be finished with receiving the waters of the rain that fall upon it. A childless couple crave a child. And the grave is never satisfied: not until every human being who ever lived has died will the grave close its deadly mouth.

And jealousy is as relentless as the grave. Where husband and wife are united in this powerful love, they have so taken possession of each other that they are never satisfied. They are always eager for more. And that is just what God intended.

So we are invited to celebrate the power of love.

LOVE IS PASSIONATE

"Many waters cannot quench love, No flood can sweep it away." It is simply impossible to pour cold water on true love and dissolve it.

Waters and floods are often used in the Bible as a picture of life's hardships. Isaiah 59:19 speaks of the enemy coming in like a flood. Psalm 88:7 says, "Your wrath lies heavy upon me, and you have afflicted me with all your waves." Affliction is part of life, and part of married life is the fact that the love of a couple is tested—repeatedly—in these waters of affliction and pain. But the amazing thing about love is its survivability. It is an invincible passion. Sorely tested, it comes through.

Of course, the love of God is just the same. The apostle asks the question in Romans 8:35, "Who shall separate us from the love of Christ? Shall tribulation, or distress, or persecution, or famine, or nakedness, or peril, or sword?" If these waters of affliction flow over us during our lifetime, will that cut us off from Christ's love? And the apostle replies, "I am persuaded that [nothing] shall be able to separate us from the love of God which is in Christ Jesus our Lord" (v. 38–39).

God is so passionate towards his people that he will hold on to them come what may. And, in reflection of that, a husband and wife are glued together in the passion of love through thick and thin. It's part of being made in the image of God.

So we are invited to celebrate the passion of love.

LOVE IS PRICELESS

"If someone were to offer for love all the wealth in his house, he would be utterly despised." In other words, you just can't buy love. It's far too valuable for that. If you try, you'll make yourself look an utter fool. If a man proposes to a woman, and in the course of his speech says, "I'll make you very rich," but never says, "I love you," she won't be very impressed. You can't buy love. If a woman abandons her husband, lured by the wealth of a richer man, she becomes despicable.

You can't buy God's love either. Listen to what Moses said in God's name to the people of Israel: "The LORD did not set his love on you nor choose you because you were more in number than any other people, for you were the least of all peoples; but because the LORD loves you" (Deuteronomy 7:7-8). The LORD simply loves. There is absolutely nothing that we can do to secure God's love. He loved his people before we ever existed. The Lord Jesus came into the world because, from eternity God so loved the world.

In the same way, a man cannot swap wealth for love. True love between husband and wife is a priceless gift. It is a reflection of the God in whose image we are made.

So we are invited to celebrate the pricelessness of love.

It remains at this point just to wonder at the love of God which surpasses knowing, that powerful, passionate, priceless love in Christ crucified for sinners, that love from which nothing can separate us. *That* is a love worth celebrating.

3

An Impressionistic Song Cycle

A SONG IS A work of the imagination. It is poetic. It's a work of art. In my opinion there is something very attractive about the paintings of the late nineteenth century artist Claude Monet. He represented a school of art known as "Impressionism." According to this theory (to over-simplify things a bit), a work of art is designed to convey a general impression, and not to be specific at every single point. Impressionistic painters had an influence on certain musicians. Monet's younger contemporary, Claude Debussy, introduced impressionism to music.

I like to think of the Song of Solomon as an impressionistic song. It's intended to convey an impression. Being a love song, the impression it wants to convey is that it's worth celebrating sexual love.

Because this Song is impressionistic, interpretation is tricky. Two people can look at any work of art and think it's about entirely different things. When you read the commentaries on the Song of Solomon, you find that there are many varied interpretations. This is not surprising, but it does suggest that we are unwise to try to squeeze some meaning out of every little detail. If we try to press for some significance in every word or every line, we lose something of what the Song is really all about. It is written in picture language. To over-explain it is to risk killing it. In fact there

An Impressionistic Song Cycle

are some lines in the Song which are quite impossible to understand. None of the commentators tell us what they mean, because everybody's baffled. But for all that, the general impression—the wonderful blessing of a God-given physical relationship of love within the context of marriage—that comes over clearly enough. So this is what we must take from the Song—the general impression. We shall therefore take the book in fairly large portions, rather than studying it strictly verse-by-verse. Our aim is to get the overall impression of Solomon celebrating sexual love.

We need to remember too that the Song of Solomon is a work of fiction. Solomon is pondering, towards the end of his life, what an ideal marriage might be like. He is thinking about what his marriage to his wife, Shulamite, could have been. But his marriage was not like this at all. The purpose of this artistic composition is to commend to every married couple what they may enjoy by the goodness of God.

So it would be quite wrong to try to find in every detail in the Song a reference to something that actually happened. Solomon is being led by the Holy Spirit to let his imagination run away with him. The result is that we are given the impression that marriage is a wonderful gift for which we should be seriously and joyfully thankful.

That is especially true because the marriage relationship between man and wife points beyond itself to God's love in Christ for his people. And when we have looked up through this description of human marriage to that love, then we are brought back down to earth again with a new determination, in the light of God's love, to enjoy sexual love in marriage for God's sake.

The nineteenth century composer Franz Schubert wrote some Song Cycles. A Song Cycle is a series of songs around a common theme. There is an artistic unity to the cycle, though each song is distinct and has its own miniature theme within the big theme.

The Song of Solomon may be compared to a Song Cycle. It is a series of episodes, looking at this wonderful gift of marriage and sexual love from various angles. Different aspects are presented. The Song is not tracing the development of marriage through life. It doesn't start with the wedding and go through "until death us do part." When the Song begins Solomon and Shulamite are an established married couple. But in the middle of chapter 1 there is a flashback to the days before they were married. Then later on in the Song we have a passage which is clearly a reference to the wedding, but it comes in the middle, not at the beginning. Solomon is not interested in chronology. The point is simply to bring out various aspects of the happiness of the state of marriage. Some aspects are brought out through the experience of a couple who have been married for years. Other aspects are highlighted by contrasting marriage with the days of courtship. Others again emerge through the excitement of newly-weds, and so on. The author wants to convey an impression, and so invite us to join him in rejoicing in the good gift that God has given, in celebrating sexual love.

4

Wrinkles and Palaces

(Song of Solomon 1)

WE HAVE LOOKED AT the key to the Song of Solomon, that verse and a half in chapter 8 which provides the only abstract account of love in the whole book. Now we turn back to the beginning as we start to listen to this cycle of the music of love.

The first verse is simply the title. It identifies the human author who composed this Song under the inspiration of the Holy Spirit. And it makes the claim to be the most excellent of all songs. Little wonder, because it is on the most excellent of all themes—as Paul makes clear, the "more excellent way" (1 Corinthians 12:31) is the way of love (1 Corinthians 13).

What impression of love and sex within marriage is conveyed by Song of Solomon 1? Five themes seem to emerge.

THE MAGNIFICENT JOY OF MARRIED LOVE (VV. 2-4)

> ² Oh that he would kiss me with the kisses of his mouth—
> For your lovemaking is better than wine.

> **3** Your oils have a pleasing fragrance,
> And your name is like those oils poured out;
> No wonder young women adore you.
> **4** Draw me away!
> Let us run together.
> The king has brought me into his chambers.
> We will be glad and rejoice in you.
> We will remember your lovemaking more than wine.
> It is only right that they adore you.[1]

In this passage the wife is speaking. She is really speaking to herself. She is musing. She is addressing her husband in her imagination.

The wife is longing to receive her husband's physical expression of love: "Oh that he would kiss me with the kisses of his mouth." She is speaking to herself, expressing her desire. Then in the second part of verse 2 she imagines that she is speaking to her husband: "For your lovemaking is better than wine." I am persuaded by the observation that "the word 'love' in most translations is too general and evasive."[2] The Hebrew word is an unusual one, and is best translated "lovemaking." It is derived from a root which means "to boil." It denotes the hot passion involved in the physical expression of love. As far as the wife is concerned, her husband's lovemaking is something she would far rather enjoy than the best vintage wine. She continues in verse 3, still imagining the delight of being with her husband. The very mention of his name brings joy to her. In verse 4 she is excitedly anticipating the next occasion when she will be able to experience sexual union with the one she loves. And it really will be union. So she says, "We will be glad and rejoice in you." She knows that, in loving each other, the husband and the wife share that love. In his making love to her both she and he find pleasure, a pleasure that is better than wine.

---

1. V. 2, line 1 HCSB, line 2 orig; v. 3, line 1 NASB, line 2 REB, line 3 HCSB; v. 4, line 1 NKJV, line 2 NASB, lines 3–4 NKJV, line 5 orig, line 6 HCSB.

2. Bloch and Bloch, *Song*, 137.

The main point of these verses is the magnificent joy of it all. She mentions wine in verse 2 and 4, and oils in verse 3. Both of these things are used in the Bible as emblems of joy and gladness. For example, Psalm 104:15 says that wine "makes glad the heart of man," and Isaiah 61:3 speaks of "the oil of joy." Wine and oil—both are symbols of joy. So in speaking of these two things here, the woman is simply saying, there is nothing that brings me greater pleasure than my husband's lovemaking.

God has given us sex and marriage to bring us joy, a joy so magnificent that it's better than anything else that's possible on earth. So we are invited to celebrate that fact, to rejoice in God's gift.

But perhaps there's a bit of a challenge in these words as well. When we hear Shulamite musing like this it makes us check that there's nothing defective in our marriages. Maybe husbands need to hear this challenge. Does your wife feel like this? Does she think that there's nothing better in all the world, nothing more happy, than your love for her? Or is there something lacking in the husband's love for his wife? By the way, in these studies in the Song of Solomon, I find that the challenges to husbands always seem to be stronger than the challenges to wives. Maybe that's quite intentional. Solomon writes as a man who failed in marriage. Perhaps he intends the Song to be a message to men. In Ephesians 5:22–33, similarly, the apostle has a lot more to say to husbands than to wives. Maybe that's because men have to work at these things more than women do, to reach the ideal marriage that's portrayed by the Song.

Now let's lift our sights a bit higher. We remember that the bride of Christ, the Church, knows the joy of his love. Just as Shulamite longs for Solomon, so the Church longs for Jesus Christ, and enjoys him above everything else. The love of God is demonstrated in this, that "while we were still sinners, Christ died for us" (Romans 5:8). Marriage to the Lord Jesus involves admitting that we are sinners, and that we need his death to save us from our sins. Then you begin a life of joyful celebration.

I have not so far commented on the last line of verse 3 and the last line of verse 4. Who are the young women who adore Shulamite's husband? I don't think that they are anybody in particular. The wife is simply reveling in the fact that she has a husband who is widely respected by others. She is saying, "other people admire you, and that makes me happy."

If we husbands want our wives to be able to revel in the fact that we are appreciated and admired by other people, we'd better live so that other people do respect us!

THE DEMANDING RESPONSIBILITY OF MARRIED LOVE (VV. 5-6)

> 5 I am very dark, but lovely,
> O daughters of Jerusalem,
> Dark like the tents of Kedar,
> Yet lovely like the curtains of Solomon.
> 6 Don't look down on me, because I'm dark,
> Because the sun has tanned me.
> My mother's sons were angry with me;
> They made me caretaker of the vineyards,
> But I have not taken care of my own vineyard.[3]

Here the wife is still speaking, but this time she is addressing "the daughters of Jerusalem." In the commentaries you will find umpteen different suggestions as to who they might be. In my opinion they represent young women in general. Several times Shulamite speaks to them. Their presence serves both to add vividness and color to the song, but also to provide the opportunity for some important teaching on the theme of sex, love and marriage. At this point in the Song we are to understand that the couple have been married for some years.

The wife admits that she is very dark, as dark as "the tents of Kedar." The people of Kedar used to make their tents with the

---

3. V. 5, lines 1–2 ESV, line 3 NIV, line 4 HCSB; v. 6, line 1 MSG, line 2 NKJV, lines 3–5 NASB.

Wrinkles and Palaces

skins of black goats. The reason why the wife is that dark is that she has a sun tan. Today, it seems that most women would give anything to have a sun tan. But as far as Shulamite was concerned it was not something to be proud of. People got a sun tan in those days if they were not of sufficient social standing to be able to stay indoors out of the sun. Outdoor work was burdensome.

But here we are dealing in picture language. Shulamite is pointing out that there is something burdensome about marriage, in particular, at this point, for the woman. There are responsibilities to shoulder. There are demands which take their toll. Perhaps to people in general, especially to the younger generation, she looks merely dark, unattractive.

But then she says, I am "lovely." To her husband she is lovely indeed, as lovely as "the curtains of Solomon." When Solomon built the temple he hung there the veil, the curtain "of blue and purple and crimson and fine linen" (2 Chronicles 3:14). Shulamite says, yes the burdensome responsibility of marriage has taken its toll on me, and that is what young women notice, but as far as my husband is concerned, I am as lovely as the finest curtains.

In the last three lines of verse 6, I think that the first two lines are really just preparing the way for the third. We don't need to inquire too closely what they mean. Shulamite's main point is stated in the last line. What that means is "I am married." The vineyard is used several times in the Song as a symbol of female sexuality. She is saying, I have given that to my husband; I haven't kept it; I'm married; that's made me dark, but to my husband I'm lovely; the responsibilities have had their effect on me, but still my husband admires me.

Every husband needs to remember as he grows older that so does his wife. It may be, as the years go by, that all that other people notice are the wrinkles, the greying hair, the stooped shoulders—the darkness. But with the husband it's different. He sees in those very features his wife's loveliness. They are the marks of a life of demanding responsibility in being married to him. She has fulfilled those responsibilities so faithfully, so cheerfully, so selflessly, with so little grumbling. At times the wife has had to battle through her own emotions to wait on her husband, when he was scarcely aware of her struggles. And the very darkness is the loveliness as far as the husband is concerned.

A husband needs always to keep his wife's loveliness before his eyes. She has not kept herself for herself. She has allowed him to possess her. What a sacrifice! What a demanding responsibility!

Now a husband may feel like protesting, but I have burdens and responsibilities too. That may be so, but it's not what these verses are talking about, so that's not our theme just now. The husband needs to overcome his own selfishness, forget about his burdens, and thank his wife for her loveliness. After all, isn't it usually the case that the burdens and responsibilities of marriage are harder on the wife than on the husband? So as far as the husband is concerned, he needs to remember that her loveliness grows by the month—and he needs to tell her, and thank her.

THE SECURE TOGETHERNESS OF MARRIED LOVE (VV. 7–8)

> 7 Tell me, O you whom I adore,
> Where you feed,
> Where you take your rest at noon.
> For why should I be like one who wanders
> Beside the flocks of your companions?
>
> 8 If you do not know, O fairest among women,
> Follow in the footsteps of the flock,
> And feed your little goats
> Beside the shepherds' tents.[4]

In these verses we have a conversation. In verse 7 the woman speaks and in verse 8 the man replies. This is a flashback to the days before they were married. They are a courting couple at this point. In the flashback passages the word which denotes

4. V. 7, line 1 orig, line 2 KJV, line 3 orig, lines 4–5 RSV; v. 8 NKJV.

Wrinkles and Palaces

admiration is used, to distinguish it from sexual love consummated in marriage.

In verse 7 the young lady feels insecure. She is full of appreciation for her fiancé, and longs for that time when she can be with him all day (and all night). Then she will no longer be vulnerable in her singleness. But then in verse 8 the husband-to-be has no option but to reply that he can do nothing about it just yet. It is not yet time for them to "know" each other in sexual union. They long for this security of togetherness, but the fiancé has to say, yes I know you don't want to be mixing with my companions, but there's nothing I can do about it: you've just got to feed your little goats beside the shepherd's tents; you want to know where I feed and take my rest at noon so you can be with me all day, but it's not time yet to know each other.

Many translations assume that the woman's enquiry in verse 7 relates to her fiancé's flock. However, there is no reference to the flock in the original Hebrew. It is possible that the Shulamite may be asking about Solomon himself rather than his flock, and this is how I take it

In Solomon's day a woman who was unmarried was especially vulnerable. There would be no financial security for her. Today, although that may have changed, it's still the case that marriage brings a sense of emotional security and safety, for both husband and wife. And we need to be thankful for that and take care not to damage it.

These verses remind us of the principle, laid down by God in his word, that sex is legitimate only within the context of marriage. It is beautiful there, but anywhere else it is filthy. This couple longed for it, but they were restrained. They knew the time was not yet.

Now let's lift our sights again. Let's think of the love of God, and what security there is in that love. In Christ crucified, the highest demonstration of the love of God, we are secure on the day of judgement itself, when we are trusting in him to save us.

Sex, Love, and Marriage—A Celebration

THE BEAUTIFYING AFFIRMATION OF MARRIED LOVE (VV. 9-16A)

9 I would compare you, my dearest,
To a chariot-horse of Pharaoh.
10 Your cheeks are lovely with ornaments,
Your neck with strings of beads.
11 We will make for you ornaments of gold
With beads of silver.

12 While the king is at his table,
My perfume fills the air with its fragrance.
13 My lover is to me a sachet of myrrh,
That lies all night between my breasts.
14 My lover is to me a cluster of henna blossoms
From the vineyards of En Gedi.

15 How beautiful you are, my love,
How beautiful!
You eyes are soft as doves.

16 How handsome you are, my lover,
And how pleasant![5]

Now we are back with the couple when they are married. Again this is a conversation. He speaks in verse 9-11, and verse 15. She speaks in verse 12-14 and the first part of verse 16.

When you read this passage you could form the impression that this couple have started a mutual admiration society! They are flattering each other with various expressions. But then, when you think about it, isn't that just what marriage is? It is to be hoped that a husband and wife admire each other. How tragic if, with the passing of the years, contempt for each other were to set in. We must never lose respect for each other within marriage. But if we want respect, we had better behave so that

---

5. V. 9 REB; vv. 10–11 NASB; v. 12, line 1 NKJV, line 2 GW; v. 13, line 1 NIV, line 2 NKJV; v. 14 NIV; v. 15 LB; v. 16a, line 1 NIV, line 2 NEB.

Wrinkles and Palaces

we deserve it. And it is good to put our feelings into words, like Solomon and Shulamite do.

Here the husband speaks first. He compares his wife to one of the horses pulling Pharaoh's chariots. Perhaps you have seen a shire horse at an agricultural show. They decorate them with all sorts of colorful ornaments. That's the kind of thing that is being referred to here. In verse 10 he is imagining the elegance of a horse when it is covered with all these things that make its beauty so much the greater. But in verse 11, the husband makes a suggestion to his wife. In verse 10 he has spoken of ornaments and strings of beads in general terms. Now he suggests going one better and making them of gold and silver. What lies behind the suggestion is the thought, you are far more beautiful than the best of Pharaoh's horses; however elegantly decorated they may be, they've just got any old ornaments, any old beads, but your beauty, my wife, is gold and silver, second to none.

It is interesting how Solomon says, "We will make for you ornaments of gold." There is a sense in which love creates beauty. A woman who is loved by her husband develops elegance, not just outwardly, but in personality and character as well. By loving and respecting his wife, a husband makes her all the more precious. He turns her ornaments into gold.

Then the wife responds in verse 12. The two of them are having a special private meal before they adjourn to bed. The meal is her opportunity to entice her husband with her love for him. Then in verses 13 and 14 we find them making love to each other.

Myrrh used to be worn by women around their necks in a little pouch. It was a solid substance, a bit like wax. As it hung there the heat of the body gradually melted it down and released the fragrance. What she is saying as she cuddles her husband to her body is that the pleasure of his presence gradually increases the more she enjoys it. The fragrance of delight in being together slowly builds up, just as the myrrh gradually gives off its scent.

She goes on to speak of henna blooms. Henna was a yellow plant which was used as a dye. Women would use it as a nail varnish in those days. What she is suggesting is that in this act of sexual togetherness, the husband's influence pervades his wife. He has become like a dye stamping his character and personality on her. She feels that he is the best of the best. En Gedi was the place where the very best henna grew in Palestine.

In verses 15 and 16 they each tell the other how beautiful, how handsome, they are. The husband sees beauty shining out of the eyes of his wife. She finds her husband so pleasant to be with. It is these affirmations which they make to each other which create and enhance their beauty.

We all need to be affirmed, to be praised, encouraged, commended, approved. If you are constantly being put down you become soured inside. Your personality becomes unpleasant. But regular doses of affirmation and encouragement make you feel sweet inside, and your personality comes out as a beautiful thing. We need to learn, in our marriages, to affirm one another, and so to make one another the more beautiful. The husband must overcome his reticence, and every day tell his wife how wonderful, how appreciated she is.

When you look heavenwards you find that God is just the same. The God who loves us is not for ever slamming us for our faults and failings. He tells us we are "accepted in the Beloved" (Ephesians 1:6). He embraces us in the Lord Jesus. He affirms us for who we are as made in the image of God and as remade in the image of Christ. What a thrill that the LORD "will beautify the humble with salvation" (Psalm 149:4).

THE LUXURIOUS COMFORT OF MARRIED LOVE (VV. 16B-17)

16B Our bed is lush with foliage.
17 The beams of our houses are cedar,
Our rafters are pine.[6]

---

6. V. 16b HCSB; v. 17, ESV.

Wrinkles and Palaces

These words belong to both Solomon and Shulamite. They bring this chapter to its end by singing a duet about the luxury of their home.

In those days, to have a house built of cedar with a roof made of the wood of the pine tree meant that you were living in the lap of luxury. Wood of any kind was so very expensive that it was only ever found in palaces and temples. Cedar was the most expensive wood of all. Of course, Solomon and his wife did live in a palace. But that's not the main point that they are making. What these lines mean is that love will transform the meanest hovel into the most lavish castle.

In America they pride themselves on the fact that some of the men who became President of the United States had a poor upbringing. They have the saying "from log cabin to White House." Well, marriage will make a White House of a log cabin. It will make a Buckingham Palace of a terraced house. Love turns life into something luxurious. The world is green, bursting with life, when you are in love.

We remember that feeling from the first days of courtship, don't we? Everything seemed so wonderful! But why ever stop? Why not luxuriate all life long, throughout marriage? There is no reason why it should be true only of courting days.

And God's love is luxurious. In the end he is going to build a cedar house in heaven for his people. And that prospect sends us back down to earth. Out of the comfort and luxury of marriage it makes us give thanks to our God of love. He has been so good to the human race as to invent marriage so that we can enjoy this luxurious comfort of being together in love.

Do you sometimes wish that you had a better house, or more money, or a greater number of life's luxuries? When that's not possible, what's the best answer? This—just keep on falling in love with your husband, your wife. Then the whole of life will become luxurious, and your heart will be comforted. "Better is a dinner of herbs where love is, than a fatted calf with hatred" (Proverbs 15:17).

5

Wonders and Warnings

(Song of Solomon 2)

JAMES GALWAY, THE FLUTE player, has said, "Man's first songs were celebratory."[1] The Song of Solomon is basically a celebration of God's lovely gift to men and women of physical love in marriage. As we sing along with this Song we are celebrating sexual love.

Yehudi Menuhin, the violinist, dates the idea of the love song in western Europe to the 1200's. He describes the kind of songs which emerged during that century as "songs of earthy and passionate love."[2] Well, the Song of Solomon beat western Europe by a good 2000 years. But it is just as passionate and just as earthy. We have noted that the love described between Solomon and Shulamite points us upwards to the love of God for his people in Christ, but it also brings us right back down to earth to celebrate sexual love in the context of marriage with all the passion of that love.

---

1. Mann and Galway, *Music in Time*, 14.
2. Menuhin, *Music of Man*, 61.

Wonders and Warnings

In the century after the love song first appeared in western Europe, Yehudi Menuhin points out, the love duet was established for the first time on this continent. He writes: "It was possible now for the voices of a man and woman to join in singing the praises of the pangs and rewards of love."[3] Well, again the Song of Solomon had the same idea many centuries sooner. Here we have a love duet—Solomon and Shulamite singing together of love, and especially its rewards. They rejoice together in what every marriage might be by the grace of God. It is an idealized picture, full of imagery. But it is a target, which we should all be aiming at in our married lives.

In chapter two there are four main themes, interspersed with two words of warning.

THEME 1: MARRIED LOVE MAKES YOU SPECIAL (VV. 1-3A)

1 I am a rose of Sharon,
A lily of the valleys.

2 Like a lily in a field of thistles,
So is my love among the young women.

3A Like an apple tree among the trees of the woods,
So is my beloved among the young men.[4]

Here is an example of the love duet, where the wife and her husband sing in turn. She begins in verse 1, he responds in verse 2, and she speaks again in verse 3. They are speaking not to anyone in particular, but just describing to each other, or to the world at large, how they see each other within the love of their marriage.

In the first verse the wife declares her own beauty, by comparison with a rose and a lily. The rose and Sharon are mentioned also in Isaiah 35:1-2. There we read, "The desert shall rejoice and

---

3. Menuhin, *Music of Man*, 63.
4. V. 1 NIV; v. 2, line 1 ANT, line 2 ESV; v. 3a, line 1 NKJV, line 2 ESV.

blossom as a rose," and a few lines later we hear of "the excellence of Carmel and Sharon." A rose blossoms, and Sharon is marked by excellence. And Shulamite describes herself as a rose blossoming with excellence. The lily is found in Hosea 14:5. Here God says, "I will be like the dew to Israel; he shall grow like the lily." So the lily speaks of growth. Taking the two flowers together, we have a picture of growth in blossoming excellence, growth in beauty. The wife is conscious that she is growing in beauty day by day.

We might ask, isn't that a bit conceited? But the answer is: not at all. She is musing on her husband's words to her. She has heard him declare how beautiful she is, and how her beauty blossoms abundantly as the years pass. She is reveling in what she has heard him say to her.

Then in verse 2 we actually hear him say it. The husband pictures an ugly scene. Thorn bushes are growing everywhere. But then he says, look, here in the middle is this solitary lily, stupendous in beauty, and all the more abundant in its beauty because of the contrast with its surroundings. Here is a husband who is aware that we live in an ugly world. Here is so much sin, so much pain. But what prevents him from giving way to utter despair as he looks at such a world? Well, it's that he is able to set his eye on this object of spectacular beauty in the middle of it all—his wife.

In verse 3 she responds. If she is unique in beauty for him, then he is incomparable in excellence for her. A wood is a scene of haphazard growth. But there in the middle of this wood someone has planted an apple tree, a fruit tree.

If you've ever read *The Wind in the Willows* (or listened to the audio version) you'll know something about the wild wood. The animals hate to go into the wild wood, because it's damp, it's dark, it's full of fear. There are strange noises. And the wife is aware that this world can be a dark, fearsome place. But in her husband she finds one whose presence is fruitful, nourishing, comforting, one who is special to her because she is special to him. The wife is not just some nondescript piece of vegetation. She's like a lily. And the husband is not just any old tree. He's an apple tree.

Wonders and Warnings

Sylvia Hubbard was a member of a Church in Hull which I pastored in the late 1980's. She was then in her 60's, a widow. I was single at the time. I once had a conversation with her in which she commended marriage to me. I always remember what she said. She said: "Marriage makes you special." She had picked up just the theme which Solomon presents to us here. When you are married there is one person for whom you are the only person who matters in all the world.

And so we are pointed upwards from married love to the fact that "God so loved the world that He gave his only begotten Son." What a dignity of specialness God conferred on this poor world of thorns when he loved like that!

There is a challenge here to those of us who are husbands. Is your wife able to muse on her own beauty, because she has learned from you just how special she is, through the tender words you speak and the considerate actions you perform?

THEME 2: MARRIED LOVE GIVES YOU STRENGTH (VV. 3B-6)

> **3B** To sit in his shadow is my delight,
> And his fruit is sweet to my taste.
> **4** He has brought me to his banqueting hall,
> And his banner over me is love.
> **5** Sustain me with raisin cakes,
> Refresh me with apples;
> I am in the fever of love.
> **6** His left hand is under my head,
> And with his right hand he embraces me.[5]

Now the wife is speaking. For most of the section she is musing. She is talking to herself about her experience of love, enjoying both the memory and the present reality of her husband's love. But in verse 5 she speaks directly to her husband.

---

5. V. 3b REB; v. 4 NASB; v. 5, lines 1-2 NASB, line 3 ANT; v. 6 LB.

Now we are taken in our imagination to a hot, sunny day, a dry day in summer. What is going to bring you delight on a day like that? It's too hot to sunbathe. You're going to look for a seat in the shade with a cool glass of fruit juice to refresh you. And, according to verse 3, it is just that sort of reviving refreshment which the wife finds in her husband's love.

In verse 4 she continues to express the same thought, but this time using a different picture. Now we are sitting, not in the shade of a tree, but inside the banqueting house. Literally, it means an inn, the Little Chef of those days, the place where travellers can find refreshment on their journey. So the wife is saying, "on this wearying journey through life there is a place where I find refreshment—in the love of my husband."

"His banner," she says, "over me was love." A banner is a flag. When Amundsen reached the South Pole he stuck a flag in it. When Tenzing and Hilary reached the summit of Everest they stuck a flag on the top of the mountain. It's a way of saying, "we possess this territory because we were the first to reach it." The husband has a flag of possession upon his wife, and the flag is love. And in that love the wife finds refreshment and strength.

So in verse 5 she invites her husband to come and express his love to her. This verse is imagery for her saying, "please make love to me." She is sick with longing for his passionate embrace, because in his love she finds sustenance and refreshment equal to that of the best food—cakes of raisins and apples. He obliges, and in verse 6 we have a description of the fulfillment of this desire as he makes love to her.

Marriage is indeed a great source of strength. When you're on your own, you may be prone to depression. You may feel that you have no resilience to face the challenges and trials of life. "Two are better than one" (Ecclesiastes 4:9). When you are alongside your loved one there are resources in your togetherness which you never knew were available when you were single.

It's just so to be loved by God. There is no greater strength. In a world where the heat of trial burns down on you, when you look to the cross, and know that God loved you while you were still a sinner, there is refreshment for your soul in meditating on that wonderful love. Married love is so refreshing and brings us such strength just because it is a pure reflection of that love divine.

Husbands need to be challenged again. Here we are listening to a wife's musings on the strength and refreshment she finds in her husband's love. Can your wife muse like that? Is your love of such a quality that she finds it sweet and sustaining? Just think of the hot situations in life that a wife has to face – the trials of womanhood, of motherhood, the frustrated ambitions, the cares that are part of a woman's experience of life. How she needs to be embraced and supported and caressed and loved so tenderly! I hope that we are possessive, like the husband in the Song, provided that it's the possessiveness of love. I don't think our wives want to live under a flag of power and demand. But if it's the banner of love, they'll welcome that. So make sure that's the flag that flies over your home.

Warning 1: Young Ladies, Wait for Marriage (v. 7)

> Daughters of Jerusalem, I charge you
> By the gazelles and by the does of the field,
> Do not arouse or awaken love
> Until it pleases.[6]

Shulamite is speaking. From the benefit of her own experience of having kept herself for her husband, she knows that this makes for a wonderful marriage. Here she shares that experience in a word of warning to all young girls to avoid sexual sin. This is the only morally right course of action. Shulamite wants to help young women, as yet unmarried, to avoid making the mistake of seeking sexual pleasure prematurely. She says, you young ladies, wait for marriage.

---

6. Lines 1–3 NIV, line 4 NKJV.

Ariel and Chana Bloch are a Jewish couple. They have written these words: "The Biblical laws . . . are prescriptive, and they do not necessarily reflect reality."[7] The Bible says that sex outside marriage is forbidden, but in Jewish society, as anywhere else, young people may be tempted to be sexually active, even promiscuous, before they are married. So this warning is necessary.

Shulamite is reminding all girls, that there is a proper time for the ripening of sexual desire. God's command is, keep yourself for your husband. So you must avoid putting yourself in a risky situation before you are married. There is something so wonderfully sacred about sexual love in its proper context—marriage—that a solemn charge against the danger of premarital sex is necessary.

The reference to the gazelle and the doe is illuminated by Deuteronomy 12:22, which says, "the gazelle and the deer are eaten" (and anyone who is familiar with *The Sound of Music* will know that a doe is "a deer, a female deer"). By referring to the gazelle and the doe Shulamite is facing the fact that premature sexual activity eats you, it devours your personality and your character. It does not please: there is no pleasure in premarital sex. People think there is. For a moment there may be. But there's no true pleasure, no lasting pleasure. There is a bitter fruit to swallow afterwards.

THEME 3: MARRIED LOVE PUTS A SPRING IN YOUR STEP (VV. 8-14)

> **8** I hear my lover's voice!
> Here he comes,
> Leaping across the mountains,
> Skipping upon the hills.
> **9** My lover is like a gazelle, like a young stag.
> Look! There he stands behind our wall;
> He is looking through the windows,

---

7. Bloch and Bloch, *Song*, 14.

Wonders and Warnings

> Gazing through the lattice.
> **10** My lover spoke, and said to me:
> "Rise up, my love, my fair one,
> And come away.
> **11** For see, the winter is past!
> The rains are over and gone.
> **12** Wild flowers spring up in the fields;
> The season of singing has come,
> And the voice of the turtledove
> Is heard in our land.
> **13** The green figs ripen on the fig trees;
> The blossoming vines give of their fragrance.
> Rise up, my love, my fair one,
> And come away!
> **14** O my dove, in the clefts of the rock,
> In the recesses of the cliffs,
> Let me see your figure,
> Let me hear your voice;
> For your voice is sweet,
> And your figure is ravishing."[8]

Again the wife is musing. Verses 10-14 are actually the words of her husband, but, as the first line of verse 10 makes clear, she is quoting him.

In choosing the heading for this section I confess that I'm using a pun. The imagery in these verses is all about spring. Spring is in the air when people are in love. And especially in the words of her husband, which the wife is recalling and quoting to herself, there is an emphasis on spring and it gives the wife a thrill.

In verse 8 and the first line of verse 9 she revels in his approach to make love to her. She anticipates his dance on the mountains and hills of her body. She is excited, and his playful skip says that he is excited too. The rest of verse 9 finds the

---

8. V. 8, line 1 LB, line 2 NEB, line 3 NIV, line 4 NKJV; v. 9, line 1 GNB, line 2 NIV, lines 3–4 NKJV; v. 10, line 1 NIV, lines 2–3 NKJV; v. 11 REB; v. 12, line 1 ANT, line 2 NIV, lines 3–4 NKJV; v. 13, line 1 REB, line 2 HCSB, lines 3–4 NKJV; v. 14, line 1 NKJV, line 2 RIL, line 3 GW, lines 4–5 NKJV, line 6 RIL/MSG.

husband lovingly gazing into his wife's eyes, staring through the lattice of her eyelashes.

In verses 10-13 she remembers the kind of thing he says in this regular playfulness of love. There is this invitation to be alone together in the springtime. Love makes marriage into a permanent spring. The winter of singleness is over. The rains, the tears of loneliness, are past. When you are in love you feel that the world is ablaze with color. Music is in the air. Everything seems green and young and fragrant.

Two things especially are worth noting in these verses. First, the turtledove is unique in Palestine. Most birds sing the dawn chorus and then shut up until the next morning. The turtledove is different: it sings all day. When a wife is in love with her husband she feels like singing all the time. Love turns the whole of life into a permanent spring-song.

Second, the fig tree and the vine are regular Biblical symbols of peace and security. This song is written by Solomon. When he was king the nation of Israel was at its greatest. At that time "Judah and Israel dwelt safely, each man under his vine and his fig tree" (1 Kings 4:25). Here is the reason why marriage is a lifelong experience of music and play that puts a spring in your step: you are secure in mutual love.

In verse 14 we find the couple in the secret place able to consummate this build-up of love. The husband is enraptured with the loveliness of his wife.

So a vision is being held up to us of what marriage ought to be, and of what it may be by the grace of God. Marriage is a reflection of God's love for his people. There is joy in knowing that you are loved by God, and the joy of sexual love in marriage is an earthly reflection of that heavenly love. In our marriages we must never lose this carefree sense of fun in being in love with each other. We remember it well when we first fell in love. What a spring there was in our step then! How we used to run together down the slopes and up the hills! What effusive silliness there was in simply being together and enjoying each other! And why

Wonders and Warnings

should it ever be different just because we've been married for so many years? Marriage puts a permanent spring into your life.

Warning 2: Young Men, Wait for Marriage (v. 15)

> Catch the foxes for us,
> The little foxes that are spoiling the vineyards,
> For our vines have tender grapes.⁹

It is not at all obvious whose words these are. Some interpreters suggest that a third party is speaking, though that seems unlikely. Other commentators go for the wife, still others for the husband. It seems sufficient to say, take your pick. The warning stands, whoever says it. The words are addressed to young men. They are warned not to defile the dignity of women through promiscuity. The warning is the same as that given earlier to young women: wait for marriage.

The fox is known as a crafty creature. There is something crafty about the young man who wants to pressurize his girlfriend into premature lovemaking. The fox is fit only to be caught, because it does nothing but spoil. The same is true of sexually promiscuous young men. They are spoilers. They spoil womanhood in general, because they convey a false impression of what women are, and what women are for. They spoil that particular girl's psychological well being. They spoil their own marriage when it comes later. They spoil their own character, defiling themselves, and undermining their own strength of personality. They spoil love. They spoil family life. They spoil society, because married love is the basic building block of society. So all they deserve is to be caught.

The vine here, as is usual in the Song of Solomon, represents female sexuality. There is something tender about it. Women must not be abused. It is irresponsibility on the part of a man to sleep with a woman to whom he is not married.

9. Line 1 HCSB, line 2 orig, line 3 NKJV.

THEME 4: MARRIED LOVE BRINGS SATISFACTION (VV. 16-17)

> ¹⁶ My lover is mine, and I am his.
> He feeds among the lilies.
> ¹⁷ Until the day breaks
> And the shadows flee away,
> Turn to me, dear lover,
> And be like a gazelle
> Or like a young stag
> Upon the mountains of cleavage.[10]

In this section the wife is still speaking. In verse 16 she is again in her musing mode, just enjoying her feelings and her memory of love. In verse 17 she speaks directly to her husband.

The first line of verse 16 says that the wife finds it a fully satisfying experience to be in love with a faithful husband. The second line adds that there is satisfaction for the husband too in being married to his wife. He is fed by the love that they share, so precious to him is his special lily. Exclusive devotion leads to satisfaction for both. The wife finds it so satisfying that in verse 17 she invites her husband to spend the whole night making love to her in his playful way, as he dances on the mountains of her body!

Some translations leave the final word, *beter*, untranslated, because there is some uncertainty about its meaning. However, the same word appears in Genesis 15:10, where it means "cut in two." It seems to me most probable that it means the same here.

Human love is so satisfying because it is an image of the love of Jesus. He says to his people, "I am the bread of life" (John 6:35). Bread satisfies, and Jesus Christ brings eternal satisfaction to the soul. In marriage we get a preview of that eternal fullness. In heaven we shall be able to say of Christ, "My lover is mine and I am his." There will be such togetherness between Christ and his

---

10. V. 16, line 1 GNB, line 2 KJV; v. 17, lines 1–2 NKJV, line 3 MSG, lines 4–5 NIV, line 6 orig.

bride. Indeed, we can say it already, because in our souls we get a foretaste of the love that will be revealed to us in all its splendor when we finally see Christ face-to-face. And we have a picture of that love in the love of a husband and a wife for each other.

As married couples, we must foster that togetherness, each one seeking to satisfy the other. Then for both, the cup of joy will be full and overflowing.

As usual, most of the application which we have drawn from this chapter is to husbands. The wife has spoken most of Song of Solomon 2, but her words are a challenge to men to be like her husband, as she describes him here. That will make our wives as happy as Shulamite was. Then we men shall be happy too.

6

Desperation and Satisfaction

(Song of Solomon 3)

"SHAKESPEARE WAS RIGHT ABOUT lovers: they have such seething brains, such fantasies. To be in love is to be caught up in the power of fantasy."[1] Those words were written by Ariel and Chana Bloch. As Song of Solomon 3 begins, we find Shulamite fantasizing or dreaming. We are back in the days before Shulamite was married to Solomon, and we find her consumed by passion, longing to be married.

This chapter divides into three parts. Two themes are separated by a repetition of an earlier warning.

THEME 1: THE DESPERATION OF A WAITING LOVE (VV. 1-4)

> **1** Night after night on my bed
> I was looking for the one I adore;
> I was looking for him, but I couldn't find him.
> **2** "I will get up now
> And roam around about the city;

---

1. Bloch and Bloch, *Song*, 8.

Desperation and Satisfaction

> In the streets and in the open places
> I will look for the one I adore."
> I looked for him, but I couldn't find him.
> 3 The watchmen found me as they went about the city;
> I asked them, "Have you seen the one I adore?"
> 4 No sooner had I left them,
> Than I found the one I adore.
> I held on to him, I would not let him go
> Until I had brought him into my mother's house,
> And into the room of her who conceived me.²

Shulamite speaks. She feels she can't wait. Night after night there is only one thought in her mind—her beloved. She is looking for him. She says that twice in verse 1. The tense of the verb suggests great intensity, and the repetition demonstrates just how desperate she is for her beloved, how she wishes she could have him with her now. But she can't find him yet: they are not married. The time has not yet come.

It may be that this is a dream. On the other hand she may be so consumed by her passion that she cannot sleep, and lies awake letting her imagination run riot. Either way, she is feeling this desperation of a waiting love.

The presence of such a theme in the inspired word of God reminds us that the passionate desire which forms part of love's craving is God-given. Sexual love is a gift from God to women and men.

Can't we just remember the feeling from our own courtship days? How tightly our heartstrings pulled! What tension there was throughout our whole body and emotions as we longed for the day when we would be fully united with our loved one! Why is it that there is such passion in love? There are two reasons. In the first place, the one you love is so uniquely special, so indescribably beautiful, so surpassingly precious, that you are desperate for that one. Second, this passion in love is partly an

2. V. 1 orig; v. 2, lines 1–2 GW, line 3 RIL, lines 4–5 orig; v. 3, line 1 ANT, line 2 orig; v. 4, line 1 MSG, line 2 orig, line 3 GW/ANT, line 4 GW, line 5 NASB.

expression of our awareness of the weakness of singleness. Right at the beginning of the Bible, God said, "It is not good that man should be alone" (Genesis 2:18)—and it applies to woman as well. God's purpose, usually, is that people should get married. On our own we're only half there. In marriage we're complete. So God has built into us these emotions that crave oneness with a husband or a wife.

As we read these verses, where Shulamite is remembering the tense and taut passion of her courtship days, God wants us, if we are married, to be carried back in our imagination to the days of our courtship. He wants to say, don't lose the passion of those days; always feel something of this for your spouse. Of course, once the fulfillment of marriage comes, inevitably the pitch of emotion gets less. It would be impossible to live year after year at the height of intensity that we feel when we're courting. But nevertheless, the truths that gave rise to that intensity of passion never change: you're incomplete on your own, and your beloved is incomparable. So never lose the excitement and anticipation of togetherness in love's embrace.

In verses 2–3 we find Shulamite, this young, unmarried woman, getting up (only in her imagination or dream), and going out to look for her loved one. She is still feeling the intensity of this unsatisfied desire. Her soul is being torn apart. But still she has to say, at the end of verse 2, "I looked for him, but I couldn't find him."

In her dream she meets the night watchmen. At that time every city had its night watchmen. Their responsibility was to go around the city during the darkness, to keep an eye open, to prevent burglaries and muggings. They were a familiar scene in those days, so not surprisingly they enter into Shulamite's dream. Familiar scenes often come to us in our dreams.

Shulamite enquires of the watchmen whether they have seen her beloved. She doesn't tell them his name. It doesn't occur to her that they won't have a clue who he is, because, as far as she is concerned, he's the only one who matters. Of course the rest of the world will be in no doubt as to his identity!

Isn't that a detail so true to life! How often a courting couple carry on as if there were no one else in the world. And how quick a husband and wife are to spot each other. You can pick your spouse out immediately in a crowd, because nobody else matters. This is all part of the wonderful specialness to each other of a man and a woman in love.

In verse 4, still in her dream, Shulamite is imagining that the marriage arrangements are being made. The end of this waiting time is in sight, and what a relief that will be. She refers in the fourth line to the house of her mother. That phrase echoes something which is said in Genesis 24:28. Abraham has sent his servant to look for a bride for Isaac. When he meets Rebekah, she "ran and told those of her mother's house." They then arranged the marriage, and before long Rebekah was going to meet Isaac. "The mother's house" was a sort of slogan for the place where the marriage was arranged.

Here in verse 4 the couple are not actually married. If they had been, Shulamite would have taken Solomon to their own house. But there is some relief for the desperation of waiting love, because at least the organization of the wedding is taking place.

What can we learn from these verses? The main point is this: God has built into us a desperate, passionate desire for union in marriage with one whom we love. Now, remembering that the Song of Solomon shows us something of the interplay between heaven and earth, we are reminded that the desperate feeling of longing that is part of our human make-up is a picture of something much deeper. There is something also in the human heart which is desperate for union with God, the God who has revealed himself to us in the Lord Jesus Christ. Without him we are incomplete. Without Christ, there is an emptiness, a craving inside us. Something nags us and tells us that all is not quite right. We need God, the God who has come in the Lord Jesus to be the Savior of sinners. The challenge of these verses is that we should be determined to seek him until we find. Sin has created a vacuum inside us, but God waits to fill our lives with his love and his gracious presence.

But then of course, in this interchange between heaven and earth, having been pointed upwards, we are brought down to earth again. We are challenged to see the reflection inside us of God's love. The desperation for married love is a human picture of our need for God. The desperation for love's fulfillment which we feel within us is the offspring of our heart's hunger for God. So human desire, human passion is sanctified, because it is a reflection of something far greater—our need for God.

So we may rejoice and celebrate this inner urge that drives us to seek deep satisfaction in our beloved. Remember, basically the Song of Solomon is a celebration of sexual love in the context of marriage. So these verses say to all who are married, cherish your spouse, show appreciation; remember how your loved one has brought satisfaction to your hungry heart, brought relief to your tortured emotions. Never lose the sense of gratitude for that. And even now don't lose something of that sense of desperation whenever circumstances force you to be apart for a while. Always be on the tenterhooks of longing for deep togetherness.

Warning: Young Ladies, Wait for Marriage (v. 5)

> Daughters of Jerusalem, I charge you
> By the gazelles and by the does of the field,
> Do not arouse or awaken love
> Until it pleases.[3]

This verse is an exact repetition of 2:7. It is a warning to young single women against premature lovemaking. It is pointing out that, if love is awakened prematurely, it will leave a girl devoured. Premature lovemaking eats up the life of a girl. It destroys. It consumes her personality, and too late she will discover that there is no true pleasure in sinful sex. Sex is pleasant in marriage. Anywhere else, it may bring a pleasant sensation momentarily, but in the long run it brings great grief and heartache.

3. Lines 1–3 NIV, line 4 NKJV.

Desperation and Satisfaction

This time, however, the warning is put in a slightly different context. In 2:7 these words came immediately after the speech of a married woman. She was telling from personal experience what heights of pleasure there are in married love if you keep yourself for your husband, if you resist every temptation to engage in premarital affairs. She spoke with happy hindsight. She had proved it from her own experience of having waited.

But here the same words are set after the fantasizing dreams of a single woman. She is desperate as she waits to be married to her beloved. In this new context verse 5 admits that the temptation to make love outside marriage is very understandable. The relief of this desperate desire seems so good. To be released from this emotional tension appears to be a very desirable thing. But here is a young girl, not yet married in this context, speaking to others who are in the same position as she is. She too, like them, longs for love's completion. She craves the pleasure which comes from the embrace of a lover. But she shows wisdom. She realizes that premature lovemaking will ruin everything.

There are some people today, just as there were some in those days, who say, if you are so desperate, who cares? What can be wrong if consenting adults do it in private? But we have to remember that the Song of Solomon is Wisdom literature. It shows us God's perspective on things. It offers us real wisdom as to how to live. It points us to where real human wisdom lies. And the fact is that premature lovemaking is actually sinful human foolishness. There is no wisdom in it at all. It just brings you down to the depths of ruin and misery. So wise Shulamite says to young girls like herself, beware of that danger; wait for the right time.

THEME 2: THE GLAD RELIEF OF A SATISFIED LOVE (VV. 6-11)

⁶ Who is this rising out of the wilderness
Like pillars of smoke,
Scented with myrrh and frankincense,
With all the merchant's fragrant powders?

Sex, Love, and Marriage—A Celebration

> 7 Behold Solomon's couch,
> Around it are sixty mighty men,
> Of the mighty men of Israel.
> 8 They all handle the sword,
> And are expert in war.
> Each man has his sword at his side
> Because of the terrors of the night.
> 9 King Solomon has made for himself a sedan chair
> From the cedars of Lebanon:
> 10 He made its pillars *of* silver,
> Its base of gold,
> Its seat of purple,
> Its inside—with inlaid scenes of love
> By the daughters of Jerusalem.
> 11 Come out, you daughters of Zion,
> And see King Solomon. He is wearing the crown
> With which his mother has crowned him
> On his wedding day,
> The day of the gladness of his heart.[4]

For all the frustrations of the waiting time, it does come to an end at last. In this section we have the wedding scene. We must remember that the Song is not a chronological account of the love of this couple. It jumps backwards and forwards. It is looking at love from different angles. So here right in the middle of the book we have the wedding. They were married at the beginning of the book. They were courting at the beginning of this chapter. Now there's the wedding. It is not chronological. It is bringing different aspects from here and there to show what a wonderful thing sexual love is in the context of marriage.

This whole section is building up to the climax of the final line. The wedding day is a day of gladness. Especially is that true for the happy couple, specifically in verse 11 for Solomon, but surely for Shulamite too, as she becomes his wife. The desperate

---

4. V. 6, line 1 orig, line 2 NKJV, line 3 HCSB, line 4 NKJV; v. 7, line 1 orig, line 2 ESV, line 3 RSV; v. 8, lines 1–2 HBE, lines 3–4 WBC; v. 9, line 1 NASB, line 2 ANT; v. 10, lines 1–3 BBE, line 4 GW, line 5 NKJV; v. 11, line 1 NIV, line 2 GNB, line 3 NEB, line 4 NEB, line 5 NKJV.

Desperation and Satisfaction

period of waiting is over. The months of anticipation have come to an end. The day of fulfillment and satisfaction has arrived. They are united as husband and wife. They are free now to enjoy what they have been desperately waiting for. The result is relief and gladness.

I want you to notice the way I have laid out these verses. The gap after verse 6 is deliberate. These verses are a single section to do with the wedding day, but they fall into two subsections, verse 6, and verses 7–11. It seems that this section represents the excited and admiring voices of the wedding guests.

Verse 6 is a rhetorical question. The answer is not found in verse 7. In 8:5, we find the same question, "Who is this rising out from the wilderness, leaning on her lover?" That makes it obvious who "it" is. It's the bride. It's Shulamite. This verse is about her. What we have in 3:6 is an exalted description of the bride's triumphant splendor on her wedding day. Verse 6 is really the ancient equivalent of that modern ditty which has been set to *The Wedding March*, "Here comes the bride."

The second line of the verse echoes Joel 2:30, which also refers to pillars of smoke. Joel is talking about signs and wonders that God will do at the end. Here the bride is being compared to pillars of smoke. In other words, when you see this beautiful bride, you are looking at a true wonder, a woman resplendent in her feminine beauty. That beauty is focussed in the sweet fragrance of her perfumes.

In Solomon's day, merchant traders brought in massive wealth to the kingdom. We read about it in 1 Kings 10:14–15: "The weight of gold that came to Solomon yearly was six hundred and sixty-six talents of gold, besides that from the travelling merchants, from the income of traders." In the world of those days, trading in aromatic spices was a very important part of the international economy. We get a clue to that from Ezekiel 27:22: "The merchants of Sheba and Raamah were your merchants. They traded for your wares the choicest spices." This description of the wealth that the merchants bring is telling us that in the approach of the bride we are catching a glimpse of something that money just can't buy, something far more valuable than all the wealth of the merchants put together. Here is a woman, no mere commodity, but someone precious, special, unique, fragrant with all the merchants' spices at once. Gold and silver are nothing in comparison with a bride. Here is a man waiting for a treasure the like of which he has never handled before.

Those of us who are husbands must remember our wedding day. How regal your wife looked then. She was so stunning in her beauty, dressed up just for you. Didn't you feel, what a treasure! I hope you've never stopped feeling that. I hope that the day of gladness was just the doorway into a life of gladness in enjoyment of your wife. Once again we are reminded that God enjoys his people. The Lord Jesus Christ enjoys his bride, the Church. And therefore we are to find gladness in our wives and treat them as a priceless jewel.

In verses 7–11 the attention shifts to the bridegroom. He is being carried in his couch, described in verse 9 also as a sedan chair, to his wedding.

Verses 7–8 describe the splendor of his retinue. All his bodyguards have turned out. They are dressed in their official regalia with their swords. They don't need to use them today, but they are dressed up for the occasion. Their normal task is to provide protection for the king at night. But today they have a happier responsibility. They form an escort for the king as he comes to claim his bride.

Then in verses 9–10 we have the splendor of his sedan chair itself. It is made of the choicest materials—cedar wood, silver, gold, cloth made from royal purple. The word "pillars" is an interesting one. It can either mean the massive pillars that hold up a huge building, or it can mean something more like a tent pole. We have an example of the former use in 1 Kings 7:2–3, and of the latter in Exodus 27:10. Here it is the thin poles at the four corners of the sedan chair, holding up the roof. The last two lines of verse 10 probably mean that some of Solomon's artistic young female servants have decorated the inside with love scenes appropriate for the wedding day.

When we come to verse 11 we discover the main purpose of this elaborate description of the bride and bridegroom. It is "the day of the gladness of his heart." It has all been intended to convey this atmosphere of joy that pervades the wedding day, the joy of fulfillment. The desperation of love's waiting time is over. There is glad relief as love is satisfied in the marriage union. But this is only the beginning of a lifetime of sexual love with all its pleasures.

It was customary in Jewish weddings to place crowns on the heads of the bride and bridegroom. That is what verse 11 is referring to. This was not the crown of gold borrowed from the royal treasury, the crown which the king would wear on ceremonial occasions. It was a wreath made of leaves and twigs. It was a symbol of happiness.

Again we remember that there is a day coming when the bride of Christ, all believing people throughout the world, will enjoy the glad relief of final union with their beloved Savior in heaven. That will be joy forever. And the reflection of that heavenly union is found in the earthly union of man and wife. As we who are married recall the glad relief that we felt on the day when the desperation of our waiting love came to an end, and love's satisfaction became our joy, then the Song of Solomon invites us to celebrate. The Song is above everything else a celebration of sexual love. You celebrate by giving thanks to God the Creator for this amazing pleasure which he has put into our human nature. You celebrate by expressing thanks constantly to your wife, your husband, for the gladness of heart that she, that he, has brought you over the years and brings you still to this day. You celebrate too by redoubling your own efforts to make your spouse's life one of continuing gladness and joy.

7

Sense and Sensibility

(Song of Solomon 4:1—5:1)

THE PSYCHOLOGIST, ARNOLD BUSS, has said: "Pleasure is available through all the senses. It may be stimulated by beautiful scenes, tasty food, sexually stimulating perfume, rhythmic or melodious music, the soft touch of fur, and the rough feeling of a massage."[1]

A major reason why God created man in his own image male and female was so that a man and a woman may find pleasure in each other. God invented marriage so that one man and one woman could discover the possibility of pleasure escalating as they enjoy each other over the course of a lifetime. Ecclesiastes 9:9 says: "Live joyfully with the wife whom you love all the days of your vain life which he has given you under the sun, all your days of vanity; for that is your portion in life and, in the labor which you perform under the sun."

We live in a world of vanity and labor because of the damage done by sin. However, there is one bright spot where it is possible to capture again something of the glory and splendor from which

---

1. Buss, *Psychology*, 147.

Sense and Sensibility

we have fallen, and that is in the joy of married love. And, as the psychologist pointed out, joy is available through all the senses—sight, taste, scent, sound, touch. In this passage we discover how all of our God-given senses come into play in the experience of sexual love between husband and wife.

This passage divides into three sections.

THE HUSBAND'S ADMIRATION FOR HIS WIFE (VV. 1-7)

> **1** How beautiful you are, my love!
> How beautiful!
> You have dove's eyes behind your locks.
> Your hair is like a flock of goats
> Moving down Mount Gilead.
> **2** Your teeth are like a shorn flock
> Which have come up from the washing;
> Each has its twin;
> Not one of them is alone.
> **3** Your lips are like scarlet thread,
> And your speech is lovely.
> Your temples are like a piece of pomegranate
> Behind your locks.
> **4** Your neck is stately as the tower of David,
> Built for an armory,
> On which are hung a thousand shields,
> All weapons of mighty men.
> **5** Your two breasts are like two fawns,
> Twins of a gazelle,
> Feeding among the lilies.
> **6** Until the day breaks
> And the shadows flee away,
> I will hurry to the mountain of myrrh
> And to the hill of frankincense.
> **7** You are all beautiful, my love,
> And there is no blemish in you.[2]

2. V. 1, lines 1-2 LB, line 3 orig, lines 4-5 GW; v. 2, line 1 WBC, line 2

Sex, Love, and Marriage—A Celebration

We identify this as a single section because of the repetition in verse 7 of the sentiment of the first verse. In this poem the husband is voicing his admiration for his wife, prompted by her appeal to his various senses.

These verses are a description of the wife's beauty. Solomon is exclaiming that his wife is exquisitely beautiful, staggeringly attractive. Verse 7 puts it even more strongly: "You are all beautiful." Every inch of her, every aspect of her being, is beautiful in the eyes of her husband. The challenge of these verses is that this is how every husband should regard his wife, and these are the kind of things he should tell her.

Notice then that all five senses come into play.

Sight

Solomon is looking at his wife. First, in verse 1, he looks at her eyes and her hair. Her eyes are so picturesque. Her hair is thick and wavy, so much so that it reminds him of looking from a distance at a mountain side where there is a flock of goats descending the hill. The movement of the goats seems to make the whole hillside seem alive. This is a way of expressing the luscious beauty of his wife's appearance.

Then, in verses 2–3, he looks a little lower, at her teeth and her lips. Her teeth remind him of 'shorn sheep which have come up from the washing'. If you go out into the countryside after a wet spell, how brown the sheep look! Their wool is spattered with mud. But go when they've been shorn and dipped. How brightly they stand out against the green of the pastures then. The wife's teeth are brilliant white. They are in pairs. There are no ugly gaps. There is one above and one below all the way round her mouth—perfect symmetry. The husband admires God's design which he sees in his wife, and the lips in front of the teeth are just as admirable as the teeth themselves.

NKJV, lines 3–4 NIV; v. 3, lines 1–2 WBC, line 3 KJV, line 4 LB; v. 4, line 1 LB, line 2 NKJV, line 3 NASB, line 4 orig; v. 5, lines 1–2 NKJV, line 3 LB; v. 6, lines 1–2 NKJV, line 3 ANT, line 4 NKJV; v. 7, line 1 ANT, line 2 NASB.

Sense and Sensibility

Next, verse 4, he moves his eyes down a little more. He finds the sight of her neck just as enticing. She is a woman of poise and gracefulness. The imagery in verse 4 draws on a custom of those days. When armies were not out at war they used to hang up their shields on the walls of their city. As Ezekiel notes, this custom created an impression of splendor and perfect beauty: "Those from Persia, Lydia, and Libya were in your army as men of war; they hung shield and helmet in you; they gave splendor to you. Men of Arvad with your army were on your walls all around, and the men of Gammad were in your towers; they hung their shields on your walls all around; they made your beauty perfect" (Ezekiel 27:10–11). Just as perfect and splendid is the wife's beauty. As the husband looks at his wife, she stimulates his sense of sight. He admires the beauty he can see.

Sound

In the second line of verse 3 the husband finds the wife's speech lovely. It's not just the sight of her lips which is so admirable. The sound of her voice also captivates her husband's admiration. It's so delightful to hear her speak

Touch

The last two lines of verse 3 compare the wife's temples to a pomegranate, a fruit with a very smooth, curved skin. We are to imagine the husband gently stroking his wife's face. It is so pleasantly soft. It feels delectable.

Taste

We have mentioned before that the thing about fawns and gazelles, mentioned in verse 5, is that they were eaten. Four times in Deuteronomy (12:15, 22; 14:5; 15:22) regulations are given about the eating of these particular animals. According to 1 Kings 4:23, in Solomon's own time gazelle meat was part of the daily provision in the king's household. It was a regular food, and no doubt had a very enjoyable taste.

Here the husband is in effect saying to his wife, you are so delightfully tasty, I could eat you! Taste is a part of lovemaking, as the husband's lips and tongue are placed on his wife's breasts.

Smell

Verse 6 speaks of the mountains of myrrh and the hill of frankincense. Myrrh and frankincense were fragrant spices. Back in 2:17 the wife invited her husband to make love to her in similar words, using the imagery of mountains to describe her body and breasts. She wanted sexual union all night. Here the husband responds to her invitation. He says, I am going to make love to you all night. The myrrh and frankincense of her perfume are so exotic, so pleasing. All night he will revel in the sweetness of her smell.

The last line of verse 7 sums it all up. Whether the husband contemplates his wife's appearance, or the sound of her voice, or the feel of her skin, or the taste of her breasts, or the fragrance of her scent, everything is just the epitome of perfection. Every sense has been stimulated to prompt him to admire her beauty.

So the love portrayed in the Song of Solomon points us upwards to that higher, greater love, the love of Christ for the Church and for each Christian as an individual. Psalm 50:2 tells us that the LORD sees Zion (a symbol of the Church) as "the perfection of beauty." That's how much he loves us. We are aware so often of our own ugliness because of sin. But our Savior's love transforms us. It transforms God's view of us. In Christ God sees us as spotless, without blemish. He enjoys us, and we may enjoy him.

And because that is true, we come back down to earth. Those of us who are husbands must face the challenge of this passage. Do you admire your wife? Is your admiration as strong now as ever it was? Are you enjoying the stimulation of every sense—and telling your wife how much you adore her? Have you got as much imagination as Solomon had to find words to express your love? We may need to find different imagery these days. A modern wife may not take kindly to being described as a tower or a pomegranate. But there are other images which are so appropriate today, just as those were then. We must let the words of praise to our wives flow freely with all the imagination we can muster, as we express our sincere admiration.

THE HUSBAND'S DESIRE FOR HIS WIFE (VV. 8–15)

We have an indication that this is a complete section by the repetition of the word "Lebanon" in the first line of verse 8 and the last line of verse 15. This word brackets these verses together. The husband is still speaking throughout these verses. But the section is in two parts which overlap each other. In verses 8–12, every verse contains the word "spouse." That fact signals that those verses form a subsection. But if we start again at verse 12 and go through to verse 15 we find the imagery of a garden. Both the first and last of these verses refer to gardens and to fountains. Verse 12 comes in both subsections and forms a sort of bridge between them. This means that we can divide this section into three parts.

An Invitation: *The depths and heights of enjoyment* (vv. 8–11)

> **8** Come with me into Lebanon, my spouse,
> Come with me into Lebanon.
> Look from the summit of Abanah,
> From the summit of Senir and Hermon,
> Where the lions have their dens,
> The mountains of the leopards.
> **9** You have ravished my heart,

Sex, Love, and Marriage—A Celebration

> My sister, my spouse;
> You have ravished my heart
> With one glance of your eyes,
> With one chain of your neck.
> **10** How beautiful is your lovemaking,
> My sister, my spouse!
> Your lovemaking is so much better than wine,
> And the fragrance of your oils
> Than all manner of spices!
> **11** Your lips, O my spouse,
> Drip as the honeycomb;
> Yes, honey and cream are under your tongue;
> The aroma of your clothing
> Is like the aroma of Lebanon.[3]

This passage begins with an invitation to the seclusion that love always demands. Most versions translate the first two lines of this verse as "come with me from Lebanon." However, I think that G. Lloyd Carr is right when he says that "into" is "a more plausible option" than "from" in this verse.[4]

The mountains of Lebanon were famous for their deep, secluded valleys. The invitation is to go there in imagination. They are not literally going to go on holiday to Lebanon. It's a picture: let's imagine ourselves in those deep valleys where we'll be undisturbed in our lovemaking, where nobody will find us because they are so secluded. Let's have time and space to enjoy each other. There is a depth of emotion in love.

But then the scene changes. Opposite the range of mountains known as Lebanon, there is another range, sometimes called Anti-Lebanon. In between there was a plain. Abanah, Senir and Hermon were on the other side of the plain. We've been down in the valleys on this side, and now we're going up to the heights on the other side. The Song actually calls Abanah by its alternative

---

3. V. 8, lines 1–4 orig, line 5 LB, line 6 orig; v. 9, lines 1–3 NKJV, line 4 ANT, line 5 BBE; v. 10, line 1 orig, line 2 NKJV, line 3 orig, line 4 NASB, line 5 HBE; v. 11, lines 1–2 NKJV, line 3 LB, lines 4–5 WBC.

4. Carr, *Song*, 119.

name, Amana. I have opted for the former spelling, in order to make it clear that this is the mountain on which rises the river mentioned in 2 Kings 5:12. According to Naaman, Abanah was noted for its freshness and for the cleanness of the waters that had their source there. Senir and Hermon are actually two names for the same mountain, one in the Amorite language, the other in Hebrew. It was the highest mountain in this range on the other side of the plain. In the previous lines the husband said, let's go deep in our emotions into the seclusion of love. Now he is saying, let's scale the heights in our love for each other. Isn't it true that you can describe the enjoyment of husband and wife in sexual love as both deep experience, and a sense of rising high above everything. The New American Standard Bible paraphrases the first line of verse 9, "You have made my heart beat faster." Duane Garrett renders it, "You leave me breathless."[5] That's the joyful depth and height, the excitement of sex.

In verse 10 we have some words which echo the very first words of the book after the title (1:2–3). There the wife spoke of her husband's lovemaking being better than wine and preferable to any perfume. Now he is saying the same to her. As far as he is concerned, the everyday perfumes that his wife uses are far to be preferred to the most costly exotic perfumed spices which can be imported from the farthest part of the world. He is so enraptured with her. They are together caught up in the joy of each other. Nothing in all the world is more exotic to a husband than his wife. Then in verse 11 the depths and heights of emotion lead to the sweet sensation of honey as lips meet lips in the kiss.

We need to keep reminding ourselves that the Song of Solomon is before anything else a celebration. We are being invited to celebrate sexual love, and so give thanks to God who created the joys of married love. We remember that the same kind of joy is found in the love between the Christian and the Savior, and we celebrate that as well.

---

5. Garrett, *Song*, 185.

Sex, Love, and Marriage—A Celebration

And the celebration brings with it a challenge not to lose our joy, to let our imagination run riot in expressing the enjoyment we find in our spouse. As Solomon knew, we need to create time and space to be undisturbed in seclusion, to be alone together, to develop our relationship and our enjoyment of each other.

The Bridge: *The exclusiveness of true love* (v. 12)

> A garden locked up
> Is my sister, my spouse,
> A locked pool,
> A sealed well.[6]

As we have seen in earlier chapters, the Song of Solomon is totally opposed to all forms of sexual activity outside the marriage bond. That is a tragic travesty of what God created to be enjoyed. It is a mere mockery of God's creation gift, and so is an insult to the Creator himself. It demands repentance. This aim to convict of sin comes to the surface from time-to-time in the Song of Solomon. And here is a further warning of the destructive evil of lovemaking without marriage. The wife is described as a walled garden whose gate is locked, a private pool behind a locked door, and a sealed well. She is not shut up from her husband, but shut up for him alone.

In those days it was the regular practice to seal wells. It was a way of protecting the water supply for the rightful owner. The owner could unseal the well when he needed the water, but nobody else could. It was the equivalent of a padlock. It was a way of keeping a private water supply from being used by strangers. This picture is being used to say that the wife and the husband belong exclusively to each other. To everyone else in the world she is enclosed, sealed, shut up. Marriage is a sort of enclosure which is impenetrable to outsiders.

---

6. Line 1 orig, line 2 NKJV, lines 3–4 orig.

Sense and Sensibility

God's word warns time and again against the foolishness and wickedness of sexual sin. Adultery ranks as one of the worst of sins, so much so that in Old Testament times it was a capital offense (Leviticus 20:10). In the New Testament too God's word insists that "neither fornicators, nor idolaters, nor adulterers, nor homosexuals, nor sodomites, nor thieves, nor covetous, nor drunkards, nor revilers, nor extortioners, will inherit the kingdom of God." It says, "Do not be deceived." It is so easy to be deceived. The pressure of this godless society in which we live makes us want to think otherwise. But God will not compromise his standards for anyone. Marriage is the only legitimate context for sexual love.

Sexual immorality is so condemned in Scripture because it is a totally destructive thing: "Flee sexual immorality. Every sin a man does is outside the body, but he who commits sexual immorality sins against his own body" (1 Corinthians 6:18). Over the years that I've been in the ministry I have noticed that when people commit sexual immorality it is very rare that they find a way back. They become callous, self-justifying, deluded, charming themselves to believe that nothing is wrong at all. Sexual sin destroys the life. It is the summit of folly.

Of course, there is a way back—through genuine sorrow and deep repentance when God's word convicts. As 1 Corinthians 6:11 points out, justification in Christ and sanctification by the Spirit make a great difference. There is a way back. It's not impossible, though it's rare. When temptations come we must resist, or we destroy ourselves for ever.

A Description: *The luxurious life that married love creates* (vv. 13–15)

> **13** Your shoots are an orchard of pomegranates
> With choice fruits,
> Fragrant henna with spikenard,
> **14** Spikenard and saffron,

> Calamus and cinnamon,
> With every tree of frankincense,
> Myrrh and aloes,
> With all the most exquisite spices—
> **15** A well, a walled garden,
> A spring of running water,
> Pouring down from Lebanon.[7]

These verses explain why a wife is so lovable. In verses 13 and 14 we have a list of spices. They are the most luxurious spices of that day. The only ones that were locally grown in Palestine were henna and saffron. All the others mentioned were imported from elsewhere. That meant that they were very expensive. In verse 12 the well was sealed. Now in verse 15 it is open—opened for the husband.

What this means is that when the wife is exclusively available for her husband and he for her, then you have a wonderful experience of luxury. You don't need lots of money for a life of luxury. You don't need numerous possessions. You don't need a high paid job. God has built luxurious pleasure into sex within marriage.

So we are challenged to consider where our values and priorities are. What do we treasure most of all? We need to remember that the best things in life cannot be bought with money. There is nothing more luxurious than love. So we must treat our spouse well. People are always very careful with their most treasured possessions. A spouse is infinitely precious. We must handle with care, and so reflect the tenderness with which God cares for his beloved children.

LOVE'S SATISFACTION (4:16–5:1)

> **16** Wake up, north wind,
> O south wind, come!
> Cause my garden to breathe forth;

---

7. V. 13, lines 1–2 NASB, line 3 NKJV; v. 14, lines 1–2 NKJV, line 3 ANT, line 4 NKJV, line 5 REB; v. 15, line 1 orig, lines 2–3 NEB.

> Let its fragrance be wafted abroad.
> Let my lover come into his garden
> And eat its choicest fruits.
>
> **5:1** I have come into my garden,
> My sister, my spouse;
> I am gathering my spices and myrrh;
> I am eating my honey and honeycomb;
> I am drinking my wine and milk.
>
> Eat, O friends!
> Drink, until you are drunk with lovemaking![8]

A life of luxury ought to be satisfying, and in the completion of love's passion in marriage there is deep contentment. You sense that as you read these two verses. They begin with a conversation between the wife (v. 16) and her husband (5:1a). First she expresses the desire to be united in the intimacy of love. She invites her husband to let her garden become his garden, as she extols her own delicious attractiveness. He then describes that desire fulfilled, and expresses his satisfaction in having loved, and in continuing to love, his wife.

The last two lines of 5:1 are addressed to the lovers. They are spoken by no one in particular, or by everyone in general. They affirm the legitimate joy of sexual love in marriage. The consummation of marriage in sexual union is God's intention, and is therefore to be made the most of and enjoyed to the full. Lose yourself, they say, in love for your spouse.

These two verses are actually the exact middle of the Song of Solomon in the Hebrew text. From the first verse of chapter 1 to the end of 4:15 there are 111 lines of poetry. From the beginning of 5:2 to the end of the book there are 111 lines of poetry. In between we have these two verses in the middle of the Song. Perhaps that's intentional. Perhaps the author is emphasizing the central importance of deep satisfaction in married love. This is

8. V. 16, line 1 MSG, line 2 ANT, line 3 YLT, line 4 RSV, line 5 NIV, line 6 HCSB; v. 1, line 1 NIV, line 2 NKJV, lines 3–5 GNB, line 6 NKJV, line 7 orig.

Sex, Love, and Marriage—A Celebration

God's gift to be enjoyed. It is to be celebrated. It is a reason to be thankful to the Creator. There is no true satisfaction in any type of sinful sex. It's just destructive. It carries people to eternal condemnation unless there is true repentance. But in marriage there is genuine satisfaction, which grows by the day.

And so we look up to heaven once more. We remember that there is no greater satisfaction in all the world than in knowing that we are loved by God and in loving him in response. God's love is seen in the cross, where the Savior carried the can for the sin of the world, so that all who repent and look to him may be saved, forgiven, and given a fresh start. The satisfaction of sins forgiven in the love of God is truly second to none. Let's celebrate that love which we shall enjoy for all eternity. Then, in reflection of God's love for us, let's seek to give and receive satisfaction in our love for our wife, our husband. Keep on celebrating sexual love!

8

Realism and Resolution

(Song of Solomon 5:2—6:10)

IN THE PREFACE TO her book *Two into One: Growing in Christian Marriage* Joyce Huggett says: "We are not offering a blue-print for a happy marriage. That would be foolish, for each marriage is as unique as the couple who unite to become 'one flesh.' Neither do we offer a guarantee of unmitigated joy. Few couples succeed in every aspect of their relationship."[1]

We have described the Song of Solomon as an idealized picture of marriage. Solomon in later years is looking back rather wistfully, realizing what his marriage might have been—if only. If only he had been faithful to one wife and not taken so many wives and concubines. If only he'd remained faithful to one Lord, continued to draw on his grace, and not gone after other gods. The idealized picture holds before us a target that we may all aim at in our marriages.

But to say that the Song presents an idealized picture of marriage is not to say that it is unrealistic or that reality is just ignored. As Joyce Huggett indicates, realism forces us to concede

1. Huggett, *Two into One*, 6.

that in the best and happiest of marriages there are times of strain, tension, conflict, and selfishness. And the Song of Solomon makes that concession. It doesn't give such an elevated portrait of married love that would leave us thinking either that you can have a completely problem-free relationship, or that the goal is so unattainable that there is no point even beginning to aim for it. It may have been God's original ideal for relationships to be free from any tension, but the coming of sin into human life changed everything. Now, living as we do in a fallen world, if there is such a thing as an ideal marriage, it must be one that includes an exemplary approach to dealing with the problems in relationships, whether they be sexual or general.

This passage faces this very issue. The first four chapters of the Song have been showing us the ideal and giving us aspirations. But now we face up to the fact that there are sometimes problems in marriages. We glimpse a marital difficulty, and then observe how it is dealt with. So we divide this passage into two parts.

THE WOUNDING IMPACT OF SELFISH LOVEMAKING (5:2-9)

> 2 I sleep, but my heart is awake;
> Listen!
> My lover is knocking:
> "Open for me, my sister, my love,
> My dove, my perfect one;
> For my head is filled with dew,
> My hair with the drops of the night."
> 3 But I have taken off my clothes;
> How can I dress again?
> I have bathed my feet;
> Must I dirty them?
> 4 My lover thrust his hand
> Through the opening,
> My heart groaned within me.

Realism and Resolution

⁵ I arose to open for my lover,
And my hands dripped with myrrh,
My fingers with flowing myrrh,
On the handles of the bolt.
⁶ I opened for my lover,
But my lover had withdrawn himself and was gone.
My heart sank when he turned his back.
I looked for him, but couldn't find him;
I called to him, but there was no reply.
⁷ Then the watchmen found me as they went about the city.
They beat me, they wounded me;
They took away my cloak,
Those watchmen of the walls.
⁸ O Daughters of Jerusalem, I charge you—
If you find my lover,
You must tell him I am in the fever of love!
⁹ What makes your lover
Better than other lovers,
O fairest among women?
What makes your lover
Better than other lovers,
That you give us this charge?[2]

Throughout most of this passage we are hearing the voice of the wife. The second part of verse 2 actually contains the words of the husband, but in the context the wife is quoting him. Only in the final verse do others appear to speak. There the strange, vague figures, the daughters of Jerusalem, ask the wife a question. It is a general question that anyone might ask. In fact, in this instance, it seems probable that the wife is really having a conversation with herself, but imagining that she is addressing other women. The daughters of Jerusalem are then one part of her own conversation in her own mind.

---

2. V. 2, line 1 NKJV, lines 2–3 NIV, lines 4–5 NKJV, line 6 RIL, line 7 BBE; v. 3 ANT; v. 4, line 1 NIV, line 2 NASB, line 3 orig; v. 5, lines 1–3 NIV, line 4 HCSB; v. 6, line 1 NIV, line 2 NIV/KJV, line 3 NEB, line 4 GNB, line 5 LB; v. 7, line 1 ANT, line 2 RSV, lines 3–4 NIV; v. 8, lines 1–2 NIV, line 3 ANT; v. 9, lines 1–5 WBC, line 6 NEB.

We need to handle these verses carefully, because it is the most sexually explicit passage in the book. There are words which were euphemisms at that time for various parts of the male and female anatomy. We shall not spell out the gory detail. With a little imagination, it is not difficult to get the point.

We begin with Solomon and Shulamite in bed. She is in that kind of in-between state—drowsy, but not quite asleep, drifting in and out of sleep, very tired but not 100% sleeping. Her husband, by contrast, is wide awake, and eager to make love. His demand, "Open for me," means open yourself to my advances. The last two lines of verse 2 are a poetic way of saying, "I'm sweating with passion." But in verse 3 she is very reluctant. She's got ready for bed. She wants to go to sleep. She's just had a bath. She's not really in the mood. She's too tired. However, in verse 4 the husband forces an entry in any case, in spite of his wife's reluctance. As a result, before long her passion is aroused as well. So in verse 5 we find her beginning to open herself willingly for her husband. She arises in her own desire, and unlocks the door of her longing for her husband. She entices him with her caresses, and her playful stroking is as luxurious as a valuable liquid perfume. We see there something of the generosity of this wife. She has entered into lovemaking, when initially she had refused because she didn't feel ready for it.

But in verse 6 it's all over. Her beloved got what he wanted, but almost immediately she finds that he's withdrawn, turned his back, and fallen asleep without so much as a "Goodnight." She looks for him, but cannot find him. She calls out to him, but he doesn't answer. And there she is left lying awake, bewildered, and feeling very much alone. The husband has satisfied his own desire, but has forgotten on this occasion that it is his duty to bring satisfaction and fulfillment to his wife as well.

This is selfish lovemaking, and while he now sleeps, his wife lies there feeling wounded. That is what verse 7 is about. This verse is not to be taken literally, any more than any other verse in the Song. It's simply a picturesque and poetic way of saying, "I'm left feeling wounded, abused, robbed."

Surely this episode is included in the Song of Solomon as a rebuke to any man who exploits his wife for his own pleasure without true care for her pleasure too. It is a danger in every marriage, especially for men who may be particularly virile. And we have to recognize that exploitation of a wife by her husband doesn't happen only in bed. Men can be very selfish in other aspects of life as well. It is so easy just to take your wife for granted, to make unreasonable demands of her, to end up just using her for your own ends, instead of treating her as the equal which she ought to be. Men can wound their wives in spirit daily, and hardly notice. There is such a streak of selfishness in men. So Solomon says to husbands, "Beware, be careful."

So in verses 8 and 9 that imaginary conversation takes place between the wife and "the daughters of Jerusalem," representing the response she makes to her own question within her own inner thoughts. She is torn in two. She is having a conversation with herself. She is wounded.

The gist of it is this. Her husband is unavailable to talk to. She can't find her beloved right now. Yet her desire for him has not gone. She still loves him. That raises the question, why? Why is he so precious, especially if he treats me like that? It's a bewildered question in the mind of the wife as she lies awake, feeling wounded and alone, beside her snoring husband. And this leads us into the second part of the passage.

THE RESOLUTION OF THE RESULTING DIFFICULTY (5:10-6:10)

The resolution takes place in two stages. Both elements in the resolution are conveyed in poetry and in picture, rather than by blunt statements.

Sex, Love, and Marriage—A Celebration

The Wife's Forgiveness (5:10–6:3)

¹⁰ My lover is radiant and ruddy,
Conspicuous among ten thousand.
¹¹ His head is like gold, pure gold;
His locks are bushy,
And dark as a raven.
¹² His eyes are like doves
By the rivers of waters,
Bathed in milk,
Sitting beside a full pool.
¹³ His cheeks are like beds of spices,
Terraces full of sweet-scented herbs.
His lips are lilies,
Dripping with flowing myrrh.
¹⁴ His hands are as rings of gold
Ornamented with beryl stones.
His chest is a block of ivory
Covered with sapphires.
¹⁵ His legs are as pillars of stone
Set on pedestals of pure gold.
His appearance is like Lebanon,
He is as choice as the cedars.
¹⁶ His speech is most sweet,
And he is altogether lovely.
This is my lover,
And this is my friend,
O daughters of Jerusalem!
^{6:1} Where has your lover gone,
O fairest among women?
Which way did your lover turn,
That we may look for him with you?
² My lover has gone down to his garden,
To the beds of spices,
To feed in the gardens,
And to gather lilies.
³ I am my lover's,
And my lover is mine.
He feeds among the lilies.[3]

---

3. V. 10, line 1 NIV, line 2 YLT/NKJV; v. 11, line 1 NASB, line 2 RV, line 3.

Realism and Resolution

The wife continues to speak in these verses. She begins by thinking about her husband. He has let her down right now, but she recalls that he is not always like that. In her generosity, magnanimously, she turns over in her mind his good qualities. In the process this passage tells us what sort of husband every wife wants.

In verse 10 the wife recognizes that her husband is second to none. Radiance and ruddiness represent, on the one side, tenderness, and, on the other, strength. That's the kind of combination that the wife wants to see in her husband. Just now the husband asserted his strength, but the tenderness was missing. But the wife remembers that it is not always so. And her very recollection of his tenderness towards her in the past is an act of forgiveness. That she can even recall it just then is evidence of her forgiving spirit.

Have those of us who are husbands found this balance? It is so easy for a husband to be strong in his demands of, or commands to, his wife. But we need to be tender and not overbearingly strong. The wife wants a leader in the home, but not a dictator. She wants a tender lover, though not a wimp.

In the passage from verse 11 through to the second line of verse 16, she pictures him. She looks him up and down in her mind's eye. The description which she gives represents the quality that she sees in him, summarized at the end of verse 10, "conspicuous among ten thousand." According to verse 11 he has the value of gold as far as his wife is concerned. He has the darkness of manliness, which she admires. In verse 12 she looks at his eyes. An attractive personality smiles at her through them. The sense of verse 13 is: "his cheeks are like a flower bed; no, not a mere flower bed, but banks upon banks of flowers with all their scent." Maybe she is referring there to his beard. In those days every man grew his beard. It was a mark of honor. The wife is

---

YLT; v. 12, lines 1–2 NKJV, line 3 NASB, line 4 ESV; v. 13, line 1 REB, line 2 REB/NASB, line 3 NKJV, line 4 HCSB; v. 14, lines 1–2 BBE, lines 3–4 GW; v. 15, line 1 BBE, lines 2–3 NASB, line 4 WBC; v. 16, line 1 RSV, line 2 NKJV, line 3 NIV, lines 4–5 NKJV; 6:1, line 1 NIV, line 2 NKJV, lines 3–4 NIV; v. 2, lines 1–2 NIV, lines 3–4 KJV; v. 3, lines 1–2 NIV, line 3 HCSB.

saying, "my husband is an honorable man." Then in the second half of the verse she remembers the pleasant kisses which she has enjoyed. Verse 14 gives a picture of luxury. Four valuable things are mentioned. She sees her husband as a wealth of treasure. Verse 15 speaks of the dignity, the grandeur of the man. But it is not just his body which is attractive. His voice is most sweet. Yes indeed, he is altogether lovely. Everything about him is attractive to the wife. That's her view of her husband.

And she is saying all that when she has just been used as an object of pleasure and left reeling and wounded! Does that not represent forgiveness? And isn't that just typical of women?

We men need to learn what a treasure we have in our wives. How tolerant they are, how patient with us! What a lot they have to put up with! How selfish we can be! Yet our wives remain faithful, loyal, loving, forgiving. Well, we must never forget to thank God for such a precious one. And never forget to thank her for putting up with you!

From the second half of verse 16 to the end of this section we have another of these conversations between the wife and the "daughters of Jerusalem." Again, this is probably a conversation going on within her own mind.

It begins with a beautiful statement. Her beloved is her friend. What a tragedy it is in marriage if sexual love becomes an alternative to real, deep friendship. That sort of marriage is a travesty of what God intends. God said, "It is not good that man should be alone" (Genesis 2:18). That is not just because he has a sex drive, but because man is made for a togetherness which embraces the whole of life, a togetherness in which there is enjoyment by husband and wife of all the everyday activities which they take part in side-by-side as friends. Here Solomon's wife is expressing the desire of every married woman. She wants a marriage that spells friendship in all the duties and pleasures of every day. And deep down, that is what a man needs too. But it is something that needs working at. It is so easy to stop short at sexual intimacy, but without real friendship. But that is a wounding experience for a wife. But here her very commitment to go on cherishing friendship is an expression of the woman's forgiving nature.

Chapter 6 begins with a question. Where is he? Where has her husband gone? Well, he's there asleep beside her as she nurses her wounded heart. And yet, for all the attention he is paying her he might as well have left home. But look what the wife is able to say in verses 2–3. She says, I don't need to send out a search party; he's not really a long way away; I know that deep down he still loves me and enjoys me, and we belong together. He's gone to his garden. We have had that picture before. It symbolizes the wife herself. He is feeding in the garden, enjoying his wife. "I am my lover's and my lover is mine." Well, there is the forgiveness of the wife. After being mistreated, she says, we are still one in the friendship of love.

Those of us who are husbands ought to reflect on the number of times that our wives have forgiven us over the years. We are probably totally unaware of many of the occasions. And yet, for all your selfishness, your wife is still there beside you. That's her forgiving nature.

The Husband's Repentance (6:4–10)

> **4** O my love, you are as beautiful as Tirzah,
> Lovely like Jerusalem,
> Majestic as the starry heavens.
> **5** Turn away your eyes from me,
> For they disturb me.
> Your hair is like a flock of goats
> Moving down from Gilead.
> **6** Your teeth are like a flock of sheep
> Which have come up from the washing;
> Each has its twin;
> Not one of them is alone.
> **7** Like a piece of pomegranate
> Are your temples behind your locks.

> **8** Sixty queens there may be,
> And eighty concubines,
> And countless virgins.
> **9** One alone is my dove,
> My perfect, my only one,
> The only one of her mother,
> The favorite of the one who bore her.
> The daughters saw her
> And pronounce her happy,
> Queens and concubines,
> And they praise her.
> **10** Who is she who shines like the dawn,
> As beautiful as the moon,
> Bright as the sun,
> Majestic as the starry heavens?[4]

These are the words of the husband. His repentance is prompted by his wife's forgiveness. In the Song we imagine that the husband has just heard his wife's song of admiration and her protestation of loyalty to him. Her forgiving reaction to his selfishness causes his heart to melt in repentance, so that he praises her to the skies.

The reason why I think it is correct to take the whole of 5:2–6:10 as a single section is that 6:9 clearly echoes 5:2. The words "my dove, my perfect one," are repeated. This is one of those ways in which the writer puts a sort of pair of brackets around the passage, as if to say, this is all one theme, all one section.

However, the repeated words are now heard in a new tone of voice. Back in 5:2 they were set in the context of selfish demand. Now the husband's heart is broken in repentance, and he speaks the same words with real admiration.

In verse 4 the husband's speech begins with reference to the beauty of his wife. What he has in mind is not physical beauty, but inner beauty, "the hidden person of the heart" (1 Peter 3:4). Tirzah is the name of a place in north Palestine. What is probably

---

4. V. 4, line 1 NKJV, line 2 GW, line 3 NEB; v. 5, lines 1–2 RSV, lines 3–4 GW; v. 6, lines 1–2 NKJV, lines 3–4 NIV; v. 7, line 1 NKJV, line 2 orig; v. 8, lines 1–2 NIV, line 3 GW; v. 9, lines 1–2 ANT, lines 3–5 NKJV, line 6 YLT, lines 7–8 GW; v. 10, line 1 NKJV/HCSB, lines 2–3 HCSB, line 4 NEB.

Realism and Resolution

more significant is that the name of the place comes from a word meaning "to please." The husband finds the inner beauty of his wife's character pleasing. Her pleasant willingness to forgive is an awe-inspiring thing. At the start of verse 5 the husband thinks over his own selfishness. He just can't bear at that moment the look of love that is coming out of her eyes. It has humbled him. It has overcome him.

So in the second half of the verse through to verse 7 he repeats some of his earlier words of admiration. We recognize the words from 4:1–3. The husband now feels the forgiveness that his wife has offered. He has sensed that he is forgiven, and that liberates him to express again his praise of her. He sums it up in verse 8 and 9 by saying that she is simply unique. There is no one like her. He just can't imagine anyone else being so magnanimous, so generous, so forgiving. So verse 10 asks, who is she? Indeed, what sort of woman is this, so awe-inspiring that she can find such grace to forgive?

What we have in verses 4–10 is an illustration of how the wife's generosity has brought her husband low in repentance, but also lifted him up again. And now he is free once more to admire his wife without embarrassment.

And so we remember again that the love of husband and wife portrayed here points us upwards to the highest love of all—that love of God in Christ for his Church, his children. In this particular instance it points us upwards by way of contrast, because there is a love which is never selfish, a love which is always giving and forgiving. It's a love quite different from the man's selfish lovemaking. We should be very grateful that we have a Savior who was so selfless that in love he gave up his life for his people. This should redouble the challenge to every husband. We should each measure our love for our wife against that perfect standard. That should lead us daily to repent of our selfishness, and give ourself in loving service for our wife, just as Christ gave himself for the Church.

9

The Joy of Sex

(Song of Solomon 6:11—7:12)

ALEX COMFORT DIED IN March 2000. I first heard of him while I was a student at theological college in 1982. Ten years earlier he had written a book entitled *The Joy of Sex*, and one sentence from it was quoted in an introductory book on theology which I was reading. It said that sex is only 10% reproduction and 90% play. I remember the college Principal saying that this was one of the tamest sentences in Comfort's book. On reading Comfort's obituary in the paper I began to understand why.

He was evidently quite a character. I was very amused by an article about him by his son Nick, published three days after his death. Comfort didn't only write books. He was also a sort of amateur inventor. He liked to fiddle with things, especially electrical things. He also loved making fireworks. Apparently his son's most famous memory was of the time when the airing cupboard blew up, because Alex Comfort was drying gunpowder in there, ready to make his next batch of fireworks! Nick Comfort says that it fell to his mother to try to explain to the insurance people that this was perfectly normal!

The Joy of Sex

Anyway, in 1972 he wrote this book, *The Joy of Sex*. Over the years he wrote two more books with very similar titles. In 1974 *More Joy of Sex* appeared, followed, in 1991, by *New Joy of Sex*.

I was interested to notice in his obituary that in the first of the three books the subject of fidelity featured at the end under the heading, "Problems." However, in the third book, written nearly 20 years later fidelity had been moved to the beginning under the heading "Ingredients."

Two days after Comfort had died I read an article by Alice Thomson which I thought was very perceptive. She notes that Alex Comfort's first book teaches that ordinary people "can enjoy sex throughout their lives, as much as supermodels and filmstars." Then she points out how, in today's climate, sex has become a political thing. At that time (the end of March 2000) the debate over the attempt to make it legal to promote homosexuality in schools as a legitimate alternative lifestyle was in full swing. Alice Thomson wrote this: "It's time to go back to Dr. Comfort's basics. Instead of insisting that teenagers learn about certain 'lifestyles' they need to understand that sex can be enjoyable in the right situation." She notes that Comfort taught that "the longer you stay with one person the more fun you have."

To this day I have not read more than that one solitary sentence from Alex Comfort's books. I can't assess whether Alice Thomson is doing him justice or not. But I certainly like her sentiments. And I think Solomon would have approved. The longer you stay with one person the more fun you have—isn't that what his Song is all about? He is extolling the fun which there is in sex as the expression of married love. The message of the Song is that, in the right situation, sex is a wonderful gift of God. So Solomon invites us to keep celebrating sexual love.

In this passage there are three main themes.

Sex, Love, and Marriage—A Celebration

THE PRIVILEGE OF MARRIED LOVE (6:11—7:5)

11 I went down to the garden of nuts
To see the young plants by the river,
To see whether the vine had blossomed,
Whether the pomegranates had budded.
12 I did not know myself;
She sat me in the most lavish of chariots.
13 Again, again, O Shulamite!
Again, again!
Let us gaze upon you!

Why would you gaze on the Shulamite
As on the dance of Mahanaim?

7:1 How graceful are your feet in sandals,
O noble daughter!
The curves of your thighs are like jewels,
The work of a craftsman's hands.
2 Your navel is a rounded goblet,
That never lacks blended wine.
Your belly is a heap of wheat
Fenced in with lilies.
3 Your two breasts are like two fawns,
Twins of a gazelle.
4 Your neck is like a castle of ivory,
Your eyes like the pools in Heshbon
By the gate of Bath Rabbim.
Your nose is like the tower of Lebanon
Which faces toward Damascus.
5 Your head upon you is like Carmel,
And the strands of your hair are like rich, purple cloth;
Its beauty could hold a king captive.[1]

---

1. V. 11, line 1 NKJV, line 2 WBC, lines 3–4 RIL; v. 12, line 1 NEB, line 2 ANT; v. 13, lines 1–2 orig (based on ANT), line 3 orig, lines 4–5 NIV; 7:1, line 1 RSV, line 2 ESV, line 3 NKJV, line 4 NIV; v. 2, lines 1–2 NIV, lines 3–4 NEB; v. 3 NKJV; v. 4, line 1 orig, lines 2–4 NKJV, line 5 NASB; v. 5, line 1 KJV, line 2 WBC, line 3 GNB.

The Joy of Sex

In this section the husband speaks everything except the last two lines of verse 13, which are the words of the wife. This verse is in the plural: this is clear from the word "us" in the first part of the verse, but "you" in the second part is also plural. However, I think it is still only the husband and wife having a conversation. He speaks, then she replies, and they are talking excitedly about the love they share. It is a plural of emotion.

In the previous passage the husband was guilty of selfish lovemaking with a wounding impact on his wife. The damaged situation was resolved by her forgiveness and his repentance. Now he has learned his lesson. In verse 11 he is no longer saying to his wife, as he did in 5:2, "Open for me." He is no longer making a demand. Rather, he is engaged in an exploration. He is assessing whether his wife is ready and willing. He is investigating, to see. The garden here, as usual in the Song of Solomon, is a symbol of the wife. The blossom and buds represent her willingness to make love to her husband. Her husband is not demanding sex, but is going to find out whether she wants to share in love's intimacy.

In verse 12, to his excited wonder, he discovers that she is eager for the union of love. The first line of the verse might be paraphrased colloquially, "I could hardly believe my luck" (if you'll excuse a very un-Evangelical word!). The second line is a delicate way of describing lovemaking. Solomon puts it like that to emphasize what a privilege it is to be so close to another person, to have such access into another person's body and life. To ride a chariot was a sign of honor. When Joseph was made second in command in Egypt after Pharaoh, we read that Pharaoh had Joseph "ride in the second chariot which he had; and they cried out before him, 'Bow the knee!'" (Genesis 41:43). To be in the chariot was a symbol of the honor that had come to Joseph there in Egypt. By using this picture, Solomon is saying that it is an honor, a privilege, to be in this position as a husband where you are so close to your wife.

Here again the main challenge is to husbands. We must never forget what a privilege it is to be admitted into the secret place with a wife. We must never take it for granted. We all prize our personal space. We dislike it if someone intrudes on that space. Marriage is a real privilege, because it involves the husband's intrusion on his wife's personal space. The fact that she is willing is a great honor.

And this doesn't apply only in bed. It applies to the whole of married life. I remember a friend once telling me that what she had found most difficult to cope with when she first got married was the loss of privacy. There was another person there all the time, and that was hard to get used to. A husband needs to be sensitive to his wife's feelings in this respect. We must count it a great privilege to live under the same roof, to share the same space, as another person. We must be ready to give space and private time when necessary, though without ever using that as an excuse for neglect. It is a privilege for the husband to enjoy married love.

The rest of this section indicates that this sense of privilege in married love is there for the wife as well. In verse 13 the husband is full of admiration for his wife. He wants to gaze on her again and again and again and again. She is so enticing, so appealing to him. But look at her reaction: "why?" Shulamite knows that there are certain things in life which are real spectacles. She would happily be a spectator at a dance. Mahanaim was the name of a place. The place was given that name by Jacob in Genesis 32:2, when the angels met him as he was on the way to meet up with Esau. It means "double camp," though here it is used only as the place name. Very probably, in the course of history since Jacob's time, a particular dance routine had been invented there, and had become known as "the dance of Mahanaim." To watch a performance of that dance was evidently quite a spectacle. Shulamite loves it, and maybe her husband is a keen fan too. But what she cannot understand is why her husband should find the same pleasure in looking at her. This is the modesty of the woman. She is genuinely surprised that she should be such an object of admiration.

Many a wife has that same reserve about herself. She may have no difficulty in understanding her husband's desire to cheer from the terraces on a Saturday afternoon, but the fact that he then comes home and wants to cheer for her as well makes her feel like asking, "but what on earth do you see in me?"

Immediately her husband answers. The first five verses of chapter 7 are her husband saying, "Let me tell you what I see in you, so that you can understand why I want to gaze on you again and again and again and again." In these verses he is looking at her body, maybe feeling parts of her body. He starts at her feet and works up to her head. We can imagine him running his hand up her body as he admires the different parts—feet, thighs, navel, belly, breasts, neck, eyes, nose, head, and hair. It's all so beautiful, so alluring to him. It is like rich jewels, like the best wine. It's all so well proportioned: "your belly is a heap of wheat" (men in those days didn't much admire girls who were slim sylphs). In verses 4 and 5 we have vivid descriptions. The wife is elegant, like a castle made of ivory. She is a source of tranquillity (Heshbon is a place name, and Bath Rabbim was one of its gates; it was a place famous for pools of water which were so still). Shulamite is stately (the thing about the tower of Lebanon was its straightness). Her beauty is lush (Mount Carmel was known for the lavishness of its vegetation). She bears the marks of royalty. It all adds up to this: what a wonder you are! No wonder that I so admire you and want to gaze upon you so much.

The husband is aiming to lift his wife above those feelings of littleness which she expressed in her question. He says, don't be so down on yourself, don't belittle yourself; you are wonderful. He wants to lift her up above those self-effacing instincts, to reassure her of how acceptable and how wonderful her personality is. He wants to convince her that it is a privilege for him as a husband to be with her, and so she begins to feel the privilege of married love as well.

Once again we husbands need to consider the challenge of this passage. Isn't it true that many women sometimes have feelings of personal inadequacy, insecurity, lack of confidence. And the husband's job is to boost his wife's sense of worth in being herself, to elevate her, to lift her up to a sense of her womanly glory. The key to that, as Solomon knew, is to speak words of praise and adoration and admiration, backed up by actions of tender, imaginative romance.

And let's not overlook the fact that human love points us upwards to that highest love of all. Let's consider what a privilege it is for all of us to be loved by God. The Creator of the world so loved the world that he gave his only Son to be the Savior of the world. Is our breath taken away by the privilege of having that love showered upon us? Or have we lost something of the sense of wonder?

But then come back to earth, and remember this, that in admiring his wife, the husband is admiring the skilful handiwork of God. In the last line of verse 1 the husband describes his wife as "The work of a craftsman's hands." Now there's a challenge to us men. For a husband to fail to admire his wife is to insult the Creator who made her. So how careful we need to be to make sure that we are admiring husbands.

THE JOYS OF MARRIED LOVE (7:6)

> How beautiful you are and how pleasant,
> O love, for delights![2]

These are again the husband's words. He is not now speaking to his wife, but to love itself. The word translated "love" here is not the same word which the husband constantly uses when he addresses his wife as "my love," as, for example, in 6:4. This word means love itself, and Solomon is highlighting the joys of love by addressing love.

Alex Comfort spoke of the joy of sex. Didn't he understate it? The Song of Solomon says "the delights"—plural. Solomon is aware that the joys found in lovemaking are incomparable. Nothing else in all the world is equivalent.

The Hebrew word behind "for" in the second line of this verse is open to several possible translations. Several versions use

2. Line 1 HCSB, line 2 KJV.

The Joy of Sex

the word "with." There is truth in that. To be in love with your spouse is to discover that love doesn't come on its own. It brings with it a packet of joys. Ariel and Chana Bloch suggest the word "among."[3] In other words, there are many delights in life—good food, good wine, sport, the countryside. But amongst them all, the fairest and most pleasant is to be in love with your spouse.

But I like the King James Version best, and the word "for." It suggests that everybody is looking for delights out of life. We don't want a joyless existence. So where are we to turn in this quest for delights? How are we to find what will make us truly happy? The answer for the married person is to be in love with your spouse. That's where you'll find delights abundant! As the Living Bible puts it: "Oh, how delightful you are, how pleasant, O love, for utter delight!" This very verse really sums up the whole celebratory emphasis which runs right through the Song of Solomon. It is an ode in praise of love itself. The delights of love are incomparable.

So we look upwards again, and remember that for delights surpassing everything, even the joys of human love, it is the love of God which is the most beautiful and the most pleasant of all. To know and to feel that the Son of God died for your sins should make you burst with appreciative joy. Never lose the sense of the delight in that love.

THE GIFT OF MARRIED LOVE (7:7-12)

> 7 That day you seemed to me a tall palm tree
> And your breasts the clusters of its fruit.
> 8 I said, "I will climb the palm tree,
> I will take hold of its fruit-stalks."
> And oh, may your breasts be like clusters of grapes on a vine,
> Your breath sweet-scented like apples,
> 9 And your mouth like the best wine.

3. Bloch and Bloch, *Song*, p.204.

Sex, Love, and Marriage—A Celebration

> May the wine go straight to my lover,
> Flowing gently over lips and teeth.
> **10** I am my lover's,
> And his desire is for me.
> **11** Come, my lover,
> Let us go out into the fields!
> Let's spend the night among the henna flowers.
> **12** Let us go early to the vineyards;
> Let us see if the vine has blossomed,
> If the tender grapes have appeared,
> Whether the pomegranates have budded.
> There I will make love to you.[4]

As far as the first line of verse 9 the husband is speaking. The rest of the passage is the wife's response to what her husband has said.

I suppose it's a golden rule that love cannot be taken, it can only be given. That's why it is such a privilege and such a joy. This section builds up to the climax of the very last line. Translated literally, the wife says, "I will give you my lovemaking"; in other words, "I will make love to you."

The passage begins with the husband thinking back to the days before they were married. Ariel and Chana Bloch point out that "the perfect form of the verb denotes a past tense."[5] The husband remembers when he was first getting to know the girl who was to become his wife. At that time she was inaccessible. That's the significance of the picture of the palm tree. Have you ever seen a palm tree on your travels? I have seen coconut palms in the Seychelles and the Philippines. They are graceful and beautiful, and so was this girl. A palm tree produces sweet fruits. Solomon probably has in mind the date, rather than the coconut, palm. So there was a sweetness of nature about this girl that the husband-to-be was beginning to admire. But palm trees are also very tall,

---

4. V. 7 ANT; v. 8, lines 1–2 NASB, line 3 ANT, line 4 REB; v. 9, line 1 NASB, lines 2–3 NIV; v. 10, line 1 MSG, line 2 NIV; v. 11, line 1 WBC, line 2 ANT, line 3 GW; v. 12, line 1 NIV, line 2 RIL, line 3 orig (based on KJV), line 4 RIL, line 5 orig.

5. Bloch and Bloch, *Song*, 205.

and the leaves and fruit begin only a few inches from the top. The only way to pick the fruit is to climb a ladder. And this beautiful young woman at that time was out of reach. Her admirer may not make love to her yet.

Here is another hint of this warning that surfaces in the Song from time-to-time. There is a right situation, a proper place, for physical love. Before that time and place come it is out of bounds.

But in the first two lines of verse 8 we have the young man resolving that he is going to court this woman. She may be out of reach just yet, but somehow he'll win her heart. And in the third line of the verse we move from how it used to be then to how it is now. Now everything is different. Now she is no longer inaccessible like that huge palm tree with its clusters of dates way out of reach. She is now like a vine with its clusters of grapes close to hand. Now it is possible to cuddle up to her and enjoy her kisses, because now they are married. And as for her kisses, well, they are like the very best wine, as the first line of verse 9 says.

At this point the wife chips in. She takes up what he has just said about her kisses. She says, it's quite right that he should have my love and kisses. And why? Because they belong together. The word translated "desire" in verse 10 occurs in only two other places in the Bible. In Genesis 3:16 God said to the woman after sin had come into the world, "Your desire shall be for your husband, and he shall rule over you." In Genesis 4:7, God said to Cain when his offering had been rejected and he was beginning to feel anger towards Abel, "If you do not do well, sin lies at the door. And its desire is for you, but you should rule over it." In both contexts the word means the desire for mastery, for conquest, for control.

When God spoke to the woman in Genesis 3, he was saying, there will be this tendency in you to desire to control your husband, but I am not going to allow it; I have appointed the man to be the ruler. In the Song of Solomon we see how, in the beauty of married love, the curse that was placed on the fallen world is to some extent overcome and reversed. Here the wife is not saying,

I desire my husband, I desire to rule and conquer him. She is saying, his desire is towards me. But, of course, in this context, it is not the desire of power and control, but the desire of love. That is the proper way for a husband to rule in his marriage—in love. And married love, when lived according to God's pattern, reverses the curse that God placed on the world at the beginning. Here the wife happily submits to her husband's desire. She expresses that submission in the invitation of verse 11, where, in picture language, she invites him to the field of love. Henna was a fragrant, pleasant, scented plant. The wife is saying that to make love to each other is a pleasant experience.

In verse 12 she says there's no need to wait, we can have an early night. In the second, to fourth lines of the verse the wife echoes the words with which this whole section began in 6:11. There they were the words of the husband. He was enquiring, are you in the mood, are you ready? Now she repeats the question as her way of saying, yes, indeed, I am. So she gives him her love.

We have spoken, then, of the gift of love. And I think the tragedy of brokenness in relationships, which happens so sadly frequently, occurs when one of the couple thinks that love is a right which may be taken. But it is not. It is a privilege that has to be given. We need to remember that in our marriages. And when we receive that gift, then, like the couple in the Song, we need to be truly grateful and appreciative.

Again God's love is the model. There is nothing we can do to secure that love. We don't have any right to be loved by God. That's why we speak of his grace. It means that he freely gives his love to the undeserving. We receive that love through faith in Jesus Christ.

In our marriages we are talking about a gift which is so undeserved. Why should any of us think that we have the right to the love of another person in such intimacy? It is a privilege. It is a gift. So the Song of Solomon says, celebrate. Thank God for it, and don't forget to thank your spouse as well.

10

Inseparable Togetherness

(Song of Solomon 7:13—8:6a)

I DON'T KNOW WHETHER you've noticed, but there isn't a single reference to God anywhere in the Song of Solomon. God is never mentioned. But in an article on the Song, John Richardson writes: "When God is located nowhere specifically, it may not be because he is *completely absent*, but rather because he is *everywhere present.*"[1] We know, of course, that God is everywhere present in our lives, in the universe. We live our whole life before God. That doesn't exclude any part of our lives, even the most private, intimate part which the Song has been discussing. God observes that aspect of our life, and he means us to enjoy it and to fulfil our responsibilities in connection with it.

When Adam and Eve sinned in the Garden of Eden they felt shame for the first time. Even though they had been naked in each other's presence they had not felt shame before. But sin damaged human emotion, and brought shame where previously there had been none. In Christ all our shame has gone because our sin is forgiven. We are free again to enjoy our humanity as

---

1. Richardson, "Preaching from the *Song*," 138.

Sex, Love, and Marriage—A Celebration

God intends it to be. And what comes through very strongly in the Song of Solomon is that one thing which God intends in terms of our enjoyment of our humanity is that the sexual relationship is reserved for marriage.

And that is where this final passage begins, as it presents the first of two themes which make up this section.

INTENSE LONGING (7:13—8:4)

> **13** The air is filled with the scent of mandrakes,
> And all choice fruits are ready at our door,
> Fruits new and old,
> That I have stored up for you, my lover.
> **8:1** Oh that you were like a brother to me,
> Who nursed at my mother's breasts!
> Then, if I came upon you outside,
> I could kiss you,
> And no one would despise me.
> **2** I would take you by the hand and bring you
> Into my mother's house
> (She is the one who was my teacher).
> I would cause you to drink of spiced wine,
> Of the juice of my pomegranate.
> **3** His left hand would be under my head,
> And his right hand would embrace me.
> **4** Daughters of Jerusalem, I charge you,
> Do not arouse or awaken love
> Until it pleases.[2]

Here we have one of the flashback passages. The woman speaks, looking back to the days before the wedding. At this time she and Solomon are the ancient equivalent of an engaged couple. She is looking forward to the marriage which has been arranged, and which will be coming up before very long.

---

2. V. 13, line 1 ANT, lines 2–3 REB, line 4 NIV; 8:1, lines 1–2 NASB, lines 3–5 REB; v. 2, line 1 MSG, line 2 KJV, line 3 GW, lines 4–5 NKJV; v. 3 LB; v. 4, lines 1–2 NIV, line 3 NKJV.

Inseparable Togetherness

A mandrake was a plant. It was nicknamed the "love plant." It was believed in ancient times that it had some association with love and lovemaking. Some people even believed that it would enhance that aspect of your life if you ate it. But all that Shulamite means here is that there is an exotic fragrance which appeals. Marriage, with all its joys, which at this stage she is anticipating for the future, already has an appeal for her. She is looking forward, with great excitement, to the day of her marriage.

She speaks, as it were, to her fiancé, of the door of her heart. It is "our door," because she is on the point of sharing the whole of herself with her lover. She is anticipating complete union. In that union there are choice fruits to enjoy. There are old fruits, because already in courtship and engagement they have been able to enjoy just so much of each other's company. But there will be new fruits as well once they are married—things which are not available until marriage comes. The old fruits include excited emotions, the longing to be together, spending time chatting, walking—whatever engaged couples do. The new fruit will be the physical consummation of the relationship once the marriage is sealed.

The woman is quite clear that with the coming of the new (the fulfillment of marriage) she doesn't want to lose the old. The best marriages are those where the emotions and activities of courtship continue alongside the physical consummation and intimacy which is possible after the wedding. It is a great shame if the joy of courtship falls away once you get married. Throughout marriage we should always be enjoying the old aspects of the relationship, whilst remembering that there is always something new to discover and enjoy in the new intimacy of relationship between husband and wife. We need to work hard at making sure that things don't degenerate so that all that remains is sex, and all the old things that we enjoyed when we were courting have gone. That's a tragic situation. The woman here, looking forward to her marriage wants to hold on to the old things as well as to enjoy the new. She speaks of having laid up these fruits for her beloved.

She has stored them up, reserved them for him. Every married couple should make the same commitment to exclusiveness.

In verse 1 of chapter 8 this looking forward deepens into an even more intense longing. She says, "Oh that you were like a brother to me." Several times in the Song the man has referred to "my sister, my spouse." "Sister" is equivalent to "wife." It is a way of speaking of the closeness of the marriage relationship. There is something special in a relationship between a brother and a sister. In marriage there is a closeness which is not known in human relationships otherwise, except in the brother-sister relationship. So here, she means "oh that you were already my husband. I can hardly wait. I want a relationship which is as close as that of a brother and sister who were fed with the same mother's milk." She goes on to explain her reason. For a courting couple, even an engaged couple, there are limits to what is appropriate behavior in public. To kiss in the street, certainly in those days, if you were only engaged was regarded as not quite proper. Even today people despise an excessive display of emotion on the part of courting couples. It's an embarrassment.

But when you are married it's different. You are more restrained anyway, because you are more mature. But further, there is no embarrassment about hugs and kisses even in public places. There is no fear or shame. "No one would despise me," says Shulamite. So she longs for that day when there will be this intimacy which she need not have any shame about because she will be with her husband. The marriage has taken place.

On that day, according to verses 2–3, it will be perfectly legitimate for her to take her man home and put into practice what her mother has taught her. She is talking here about enjoying the spiced wine and the fruit juice of sexual love. This will be the reality which is described in 2:6. There, speaking as a woman already married, she says, "His left hand is under my head, and with his right hand he embraces me." Here she is looking back to how she was thinking before they were married. Then she was looking forward to that sexual embrace. That was how it would

Inseparable Togetherness

be if only they were married. They weren't yet, but that is how it was going to be.

We have come across the mother's house before (3:4). It is the place where the wedding arrangements were finalized. Here, however, it is the mother's role as teacher which is highlighted. Part of the finalizing of the marriage arrangements involved the mother's teaching about the life of a wife, about the desire, the submission, and all that is involved in marriage for a woman. Shulamite is looking forward to the day when that teaching can be put into practice.

There is something worth noting there. Solomon is assuming that the responsibility for sex education is parental. As always, God's wisdom is beyond question. Our society has given the responsibility for sex education by and large to others than parents. And perhaps we are reaping the consequences of that these days. Throughout Scripture the responsibility for the education of children belongs to parents. That is not necessarily an argument against schools, though there is much to be said for the Home Education movement. It is, however, a plea to remember that the authority of a school is the delegated authority of parents. A school has no independent authority beyond that. A school is a request which parents make for help in a task which they cannot perform entirely on their own. It is a parents' co-operative. But there are some things which are best left to be dealt with at home, and one of them is sex education. Maybe there would be far fewer moral problems in society if it were the mothers who instructed, rather than somebody else.

So here is the engaged young woman musing in anticipation of how it will be once they are married, and how it would be now if they were already married, and thinking, "O that it were so." But in verse 4 she recognizes that it's not like that yet. Here is a third repetition of this warning against premature lovemaking. Premature lovemaking does not please. It brings displeasure with it. Here she speaks to herself as one of the daughters of Jerusalem. She is saying to herself, as an engaged woman, "Be careful; don't let yourself be carried away to your own ruin; the day for the fulfillment of married love is not yet, because you are still only engaged."

However, the happy day comes at last, which brings us to the second theme of this section.

TOGETHER AT LAST (8:5-6A)

The first part of verse 5 gives us the briefest snippet of a wedding scene. A wedding guest exclaims:

> Who is this rising out of the wilderness,
> Leaning on her lover?[3]

Now the two are united. Now the wedding has taken place. She is leaning upon him without any embarrassment. No one despises her. They are man and wife.

In the rest of verse 5 and the first part of verse 6 the wife speaks of what follows:

> **5B** Under the apple tree I aroused you.
> It was there your mother was in labor with you;
> There she went into labor and gave birth to you!
> **6A** Set me as a seal upon your heart,
> As a seal upon your arm.[4]

The wedding night is described in verse 5. She has awakened his desire. Her very attractiveness, her beauty has awakened her husband's desire for intimate union with her. Back in 2:3 the husband was himself the apple tree. Now she says, I am under the apple tree, awakening his desire. It's a delicate picture of lovemaking. It's the very same activity that brought him into being in the first place. "There" refers not to the identical place, but to the identical activity.

---

3. Line 1 orig, line 2 NIV.
4. V. 5b, line 1 WBC, line 2 REB, line 3 GW; v. 6a NKJV.

Inseparable Togetherness

But the vital thing about marriage is referred to in verse 6. The wife is saying, now that the wedding has taken place, we are inseparable. A seal stamped an item as belonging to a particular person. To describe herself in these terms, is a way in which the wife says, you belong to me, we belong together. There is total belonging, complete sharing, unrestricted access into each other's presence, because we belong as man and wife. Before my wife and I got married, Paul Cook, the pastor who conducted our wedding, said to us, "Marriage is the total end of the single life." Once you are married everything changes. You are two not one. Life is shared in every aspect. And that is what Shulamite is saying here. The wedding vows have been made, and the two are bound together for life. That is true both in private ("a seal upon your heart"—invisible), and in public ("a seal upon your arm"—visible). Both in the secret life of the husband and wife alone, and in their joint life lived out in the world, the single life is over. When this total belonging has taken place, then whether you are at home alone, or whether you are mixing in company, you belong together, and nothing can separate you. And there is no shame in that, no embarrassment about being together in public.

Maybe there is a note of warning here too. I once read a report on a study by some psychologists. They had concluded that an early sign of a marriage in difficulty is seen in facial expression. When one of the couple says something, the face of the other expresses disgust. Or one of the couple does something, and in the face of the other you can see disdain.

We are reminded here that in this relationship of total belonging to each other mutual respect is vital. We must never lose the ability to go on gazing starry eyed at our loved one, however old we get. There is no embarrassment whatsoever about being together, accepting one another. There must be no disdain or disgust at what our spouse does. This is what the Song of Solomon calls us to aim at.

Again this Song points us upwards to the higher love, the highest love of all—God's inseparable commitment to us, his people. The thing about God's love is that he will never abandon his own. And that challenges us to be committed to him with lifelong commitment. That's what being a Christian in love with the Lord really means.

And when we feel the power of God's commitment to his people, evoking commitment from us to him, then we can come back down to earth, and seek to put the same thing into practice in our marriages. This sense of inseparability linked with the fulfillment of physical desire springs from the joy of married love.

The rest of verse 6 and verse 7 we have looked at already. That's where we began, because we saw that little paragraph as an abstract summary of what the Song is all about. It is not talking about the particular love of Solomon and Shulamite as the rest of the book to this point has done. It speaks of love in general. So the first two lines of verse 6 are the point at which the Song of Solomon reaches its climax. They are the last words spoken by Solomon and Shulamite. The climax is reached in this statement that we are inseparable now; we belong. That is the heart of what marriage is all about.

11

Royalty for Everyone

(Song of Solomon 8:8–14)

VERSES 8-14, FORM A sort of appendix. In the first two verses we hear the voice of a man.

> ⁸ We have a little sister,
> And she has no breasts.
> What shall we do for our sister
> In the day when she is spoken for?
> ⁹ If she is a wall,
> We will build upon her
> A palace of silver.
> If she is a door,
> We will enclose her
> With panels of cedar.[1]

This is a new voice, another man. No longer is Solomon the speaker. In verse 11 this man talks about Solomon, and in verse 12 he speaks to Solomon. This is someone we have not heard before. Who is he? He is any man. The appendix is telling us that what has been described in the relationship between King

---

1. V. 8 NKJV; v. 9, lines 1–3 JB, lines 4–6 NIV.

Solomon and his Shulamite from 1:2 to 8:6 may be the experience of any man and woman. The speaker is a representative of men and women in general. The joy of marriage which has been described in this royal relationship is for anyone.

In verse 8 the man uses the plural of excitement. He is looking forward to his marriage. He refers to his fiancée. We have seen how "sister" in the Song is equivalent to "wife." By speaking of a "little sister," this man means that she is not yet his wife. She is not literally without breasts, but they are not yet available for the man's pleasure. However, the day will come when she will be spoken for, when this engaged couple will be united in marriage, just as Solomon and Shulamite are.

The question at the end of verse 8 is answered by verse 9. What the husband will do is to regard his new wife as an object of exquisite beauty. Silver and cedar are ornamental. They are decorative. They speak of beauty. Of course this man already knows that his fiancée is beautiful, but when they are married he will appreciate her all the more. In the sexual intimacy of marriage her beauty will be enhanced beyond what is permissible during engagement.

Moreover, the man appreciates that his admiration of his lady's beauty will be redoubled by the confidence that she is a wall against other men, but an open doorway through which he may enter. She will preserve her sexual integrity and her fidelity in marriage.

In verse 10 the woman echoes the same sentiments.

> I am a wall,
> And my breasts like towers;
> So in his eyes I have become
> Like one who finds peace.[2]

This woman represents any woman. She agrees that she is a wall against others. But for her husband to go through the doorway spells peace. So here she is, describing the time when they are married. In verses 8–9 the man says, we are not yet married,

2. Lines 1–2 NKJV, lines 3–4 HCSB.

but what will it be like when we are! Here the wife speaks, saying, this is what it is like, because now we are married at last.

The last line of the verse is a bit ambiguous in the Hebrew. It may mean either that she found peace in him, or that she was a source of peace to him. Very probably the writer intended it to be ambiguous because both are true. He decided, poetically, to economize on words and just use one phrase to say both things. The joy of marriage is peace for both husband and wife in each other's company. In the Bible peace is a larger concept than we think of today. It includes harmony, contentment, satisfaction, joy. All that is in marriage, for anyone.

In verses 11 and 12 the man speaks again.

> **11** Solomon had a vineyard at Baal Hamon;
> He leased the vineyard to keepers,
> Everyone was to bring for its fruit
> A thousand pieces of silver.
> **12** My own vineyard is before me.
> Keep your thousand, Solomon,
> And pay two hundred to those who must guard the fruit.[3]

The man looks at Solomon, about whom the Song has spoken. Baal Hamon sounds like a place name. However, there is no known place with that name. Probably it is a fictional place name, and its significance is in what it means. Baal Hamon means "lord of great wealth." That is certainly a true description of Solomon if ever there was one. He was a very wealthy king. He had a lavish lifestyle.

But the problem with the lavish lifestyle of the palace was that the vineyard had to be leased to keepers. In the Song, the vineyard refers to the wife in her sexual attractiveness. That very intimate part of the life of the royal couple has been in the care of other people. The keepers may be compared to ladies-in-waiting. They had the responsibility of preparing Shulamite for Solomon's love, for dressing her up in all her finery to be the alluring sexual attraction that Solomon finds her to be.

The thousand silver coins represents great wealth. Isaiah 7:23 uses a similar picture when talking about a coming day

---

3. V. 11, lines 1–2 NKJV, lines 3–4 RIL; v. 12, line 1 NKJV, lines 2–3 A NT.

of judgement: "It shall happen in that day, that wherever there could be a thousand vines worth a thousand shekels of silver, it will be for briars and thorns." A thousand shekels of silver was a huge income from a vineyard. It represented great wealth. And here is Solomon, the lord of great wealth, finding a wealth of pleasure in his vineyard, his wife. But all the same there were ladies-in-waiting who had to be paid with a few hundred silver coins for their work, as they did their bit to enhance the love life of Solomon and Shulamite.

This young man is saying, Solomon you can keep your wealth. My own vineyard is before me. I have no envy of the rich and the famous and the royals. This is the real message of the Song of Solomon: this experience of inseparability and joy in sexual love in marriage is not just the privilege of royalty. It is for every man and every woman. Anyone may know the joyful wonder, the intense pleasure, of this gracious gift of a loving God.

How we need to hear this today. So many people seem to think, or seem to have been made to feel, that they have to live up to some sexual ideal that's modeled by the stars, pop stars, film stars, or sport stars, or by the royal family, or the fashion designers. But the Song of Solomon says, No; just be yourselves, and enjoy yourselves in your own way, because sex is God's gift to everybody.

And this reminds us that the model is not the actresses and the pop stars and the royalty, but God himself. He modeled self-giving love in sending his Son into the world because of the guilt of the world's sin. That is the love which we should seek to reflect in our marriages, when we give ourselves devotedly to each other.

And that's where the Song finishes in the final two verses.

> **13** You who dwell in the gardens,
> The companions listen for your voice—
> Let me hear it!
>
> **14** Make haste, my lover,
> And be like a gazelle
> Or like a young stag
> Upon the mountains of spices.[4]

4. V. 13 NKJV; v. 14, line 1 NKJV/NIV, lines 2–3 NIV, line 4 NKJV.

Royalty for Everyone

This other happy couple are nowhere near as wealthy as Solomon and Shulamite, but they are no less happy. This other couple could be you. Here they invite each other into the playful unity of sexual love.

In verse 13 the husband speaks to the wife, and invites her to speak, because he so loves to hear her voice. "Companions" is an exaggerated way of saying "I"—I'm your companion. He addresses his wife as the one who dwells in the gardens, the garden of love, the place where she is at home, the place where he loves to be with her. He wants to hear her voice. That expression is shorthand for total oneness. The husband is saying, let's be together, let's enjoy each other.

Then in verse 14 she responds. She uses the same language that Shulamite used earlier on. The word "make haste" is most often used for running away from an enemy. It speaks of desperation. Well, she is saying, let's have the same desperation in our longing for togetherness. Come and be eaten up by love on the spicy mountains of my body.

So the fact is (and this is where the Song leaves us) that you do not have to be royalty to have that ornamented life described in verse 9. The silver and the cedar can be ours, whoever we are. At the wedding of Prince William and Kate Middleton in April, 2011, Richard Chartres, the Bishop of London, said, "In a sense every wedding is a royal wedding with the bride and groom as king and queen of creation." He was right—as Solomon recognized centuries ago: true love will turn every marriage into a royal wedding.

And as we enjoy marriage, part of God's purpose is that our appetite should be whetted for that day when Christ shall be forever united with his bride, the Church. In loving each other within the context of marriage we learn a little more of how Christ loves us, and how we are to love him in response. So let's be celebrating sexual love

Bibliography

WORKS REFERRED TO IN THE FOOTNOTES

Bloch, Ariel, and Chana. *The Song of Songs: a New Translation with an Introduction and Commentary*. Berkeley: University of California Press, 1995.
Buss, Arnold H. *Psychology: Man in Perspective*. Chichester: Wiley, 1973.
Carr, G. Lloyd. *The Song of Solomon*. Leicester: IVP, 1984.
Free Church of Scotland. "John Murray: A Book Review and Some Letters." In *The Monthly Record*, March, 1983, 51–53.
Garrett, Duane, and Paul R. House. *Word Biblical Commentary, Vol. 23B: Song of Songs and Lamentations*. Dallas: Word, 2004.
Huggett, Joyce. *Two into One: Growing in Christian Marriage*. Leicester: IVP, 1981.
Mann, William, and James Galway. *Music in Time*. London: Mitchell Beazley, 1982.
Menuhin, Yehudi, and Curits Wheeler Davis. *The Music of Man*. Toronto: Methuen, 1979.
Richardson, John P. "Preaching from the *Song of Songs*? Allegory Revisited." *Churchman* Vol. 108, No. 2 (1994), 135–142.

OTHER WORKS CONSULTED

Balchin, John A. "The Song of Solomon." In *The New Bible Commentary Revised*, edited by Donald Guthrie and J. Alec Motyer, 579–87. Leicster: IVP, 1970.
Brooks, Richard S. *Song of Songs*. Fearn: Christian Focus, 1999.
Burrowes, George. *A Commentary upon the Song of Solomon*. 1853. Reprint, London: Banner of Truth, 1958.
Durham, James. *An Exposition of the Song of Solomon*. 1840. Reprint, Edinburgh: Banner of Truth, 1982.
Gledhill, Tom. *The Message of the Song of Songs*. Leicester: IVP, 1994.

Bibliography

Martin, George Currie. "Proverbs, Ecclesiastes, Song of Songs." In *The Century Bible*, edited by Walter F. Adeney, Vol. 7, 1–364. London: Caxton, 1904–13.
Still, William. *Song of Solomon*. Aberdeen: Didasko, 1971.
Taylor, J. Hudson. *Union and Communion*. 1894. Reprint, London: OMF, 1967.

www.ingramcontent.com/pod-product-compliance
Lightning Source LLC
Chambersburg PA
CBHW072009090426
42734CB00033B/2323